PRAYERS
OF THE
FAITHFUL

D1258573

PRAYERS
OF THE
FAITHFUL

For Sundays, Feasts, and Seasons

HUGH MCGINLAY

PAULIST PRESS
New York/Mahwah, N.J.

Cover and book design by Lynn Else

Library of Congress Cataloging-in-Publication Data

McGinlay, Hugh.
    Prayers of the faithful : for Sundays, feasts, and seasons / Hugh McGinlay.
        p. cm.
    ISBN 0-8091-4426-3 (alk. paper)
    1. Catholic Church—Prayer-books and devotions–English. 2. Church year—Prayer-books and devotions—English. 3. Prayers. I. Title.
    BX2170.C55M395 2006
    264′.027—dc22

                                                                                            2006016476

Published by Paulist Press
997 Macarthur Boulevard
Mahwah, New Jersey 07430

www.paulistpress.com

Printed and bound in the
United States of America

CONTENTS

INTRODUCTION

These Prayers of the Faithful were originally written for use in my local congregation. They have been modified over the years but the decision to reissue them in a single volume has provided the opportunity for me to revise them radically in an effort to improve their faithfulness to the original biblical texts used at Mass.

The format of the prayers is simple. As a general rule, the four prayers pick up some of the themes of each of the three readings. The first and second prayers relate to the first and second readings of the Mass. The third and fourth prayers reflect some teaching from the gospel of the day. Exceptions occasionally happen on major festivals of the church's year when the themes of the festival are reflected in each of the four prayers.

In writing the prayers, I have tried to highlight scripture in a way that makes it accessible in a prayer format. I also wanted the prayers to echo the readings proclaimed earlier in the Liturgy of the Word and reinforced by the preaching of the word. Inclusive language has been used as much as possible while remaining faithful to a tradition that has at its heart faith in God revealed as Father, Son, and Holy Spirit.

The layout of the prayers is deliberate. The use of "sense lines" suggests a slight pause at the end of each line, helping the congregation understand the meaning of the prayer.

The prayers are not exhaustive for the Sunday or feast day. Obviously, there will be other petitions—local and universal—and parishes and schools will have their own concerns to mention. Congregations will also have a variety of responses (sung as well as spoken) to replace the formal "Lord, hear us" that I have used here.

I gratefully acknowledge the many people who have encouraged me in this task, especially the priests and pastoral associates of my own congregation; Sister Helen Duffy, RSM, was invaluable in the early stages of the revision. My special thanks are reserved for my wife, Andrea, for her constant support and encouragement in this undertaking.

Hugh McGinlay

THE SEASON OF ADVENT

ADVENT 1   YEAR A

Priest/Leader

"The Son of man is coming
at an unexpected hour."
God's word urges us to prepare for the Lord's
    coming.
In a spirit of hope and fear,
we bring our needs before the Lord.

1. For the gift of God's peace.
(pause)
"Nation shall not lift up sword against nation,"
says the Lord.
May we be moved by the promises of God
to work for peace in our world
and to long for the inner joy
that comes from doing what God wants.
Lord, hear us.

2. For a desire to welcome the Christ.
(pause)
"Salvation is nearer to us now," says St. Paul,
and we ask for the gift of being ready
to welcome Christ into our hearts,
deepening our desire
to live by the gospel.
Lord, hear us.

3. For faith in God's providence.
(pause)
Jesus commands us to stay awake,
alert to the signs of his coming.
May we so live by gospel teaching
that we may always be prepared
for God's coming into our lives.
Lord, hear us.

4. For the gift of repentance.
(pause)
As we prepare for the coming of the Christ,
may we be conscious of what we value in life;
and may we resolve in this time of Advent
to be faithful followers of the Lord,
waiting for his coming into our lives.
Lord, hear us.

Priest/Leader

God of the promises,
you teach us to hold on to what is true.
Grant what we need to be faithful followers of
    your Son.
We ask this through Christ our Lord. Amen.

ADVENT 2   YEAR A

Priest/Leader

"Prepare the way of the Lord."
God's word has been broken for us
and its message calls for repentance.
In a spirit of renewal
we turn to the Lord
for our needs in the church and in the world.

1. For a spirit of wonder at God's coming.
(pause)
The scriptures astonish us
with signs of God's coming.
May we be filled with confidence
at the wonders of our God
as we prepare a way for the Lord.
Lord, hear us.

2. For the gift of hope.
(pause)
May we be people of hope,
confessing God's power to fulfill the ancient
    promises;
and may we so forgive and accept one another
that God may be glorified
and Jesus proclaimed in our lives.
Lord, hear us.

3. For a sense of repentance.
(pause)
John the Baptist proclaims a message
that demands obedience to the teaching of
    the Lord.
May we resolve in this time of Advent
to be guided by gospel values
and to live the way of Jesus.
Lord, hear us.

4. For an understanding of what is important in life.
(*pause*)
As we prepare for Christmas,
may we take to heart
the preaching of the Baptist,
examining ourselves in the light of his teaching
to learn what is of lasting value in God's sight.
Lord, hear us.

Priest/Leader

God of the promises,
you fill us with hope and expectancy at this time.
Help us appreciate what is important in life
and grant what we need
through Christ our Lord. Amen.

ADVENT 3   YEAR A

Priest/Leader

"Blessed is anyone who takes no offense at me."
During the season of Advent,
God's word brings comfort and challenge.
Nourished by its teaching,
we turn to our God with all our needs.

1. For courage to follow the Lord.
(*pause*)
In this time of Advent,
the scriptures alert us
to the wonders of our God.
May its teaching give us courage and comfort
as we wait for God's coming into our lives.
Lord, hear us.

2. For patience in this time of waiting.
(*pause*)
In this time of Advent,
may we not lose heart
but be patient as we wait for the Lord,
knowing that our faith is not based on empty
        promises
but on the powerful word of our loving God.
Lord, hear us.

3. For a strengthening of our faith.
(*pause*)
In this time of Advent,

may we recall the example of John the Baptist,
who pointed to Jesus as the Messiah of God.
May we be a people strong in faith
and living as the Lord commands.
Lord, hear us.

4. For a desire to prepare the way of the Lord.
(*pause*)
In this time of Advent,
may we be a people of the Way,
determined to spread the good news of the Christ
by lives that reflect his care
for those in need in our communities.
Lord, hear us.

Priest/Leader

Eternal God,
you care for us in every age.
In the time of Advent
teach us about what is of lasting value in life
and grant what we need
through Christ our Lord. Amen.

ADVENT 4   YEAR A

Priest/Leader

"The young woman…shall name him Immanuel,"
God with us.
The word of God has been broken for us
and nourishes us with its good news.
As we wait for the Lord's coming
we turn to our God for our needs
in the church and in the world.

1. For an openness to what God wants.
(*pause*)
Immanuel was God's sign to the House of David.
May we be alert to the signs God sends us,
striving to discover what God wants
for the church and for the world,
and eager to do what God commands.
Lord, hear us.

2. For a desire to preach the good news.
(*pause*)
Like Paul, we are called to preach the good news
promised long ago through the ancient prophecies.

May our lives reflect the teaching of the gospel
by our integrity, our honesty,
and our faithfulness to the example of Jesus.
Lord, hear us.

3. For a sense of what is important at Christmas.
(*pause*)
As we prepare to celebrate Jesus' birth,
may we deepen our awareness of God's justice;
and may we be guided in our lives
not by what the world expects
but by what the gospel demands.
Lord, hear us.

4. For an appreciation of God with us.
(*pause*)
In these last days of Advent,
may we be filled with joy and peace.
Like Joseph, may we have confidence in God,
trusting our God to care for us
all the days of our life.
Lord, hear us.

Priest/Leader

God of all goodness,
you are with your people always.
Fill us with your peace at this time
and make us worthy to celebrate the birth of
    your Son.
We ask this through Christ our Lord. Amen.

ADVENT 1   YEAR B

Priest/Leader

"Beware, keep alert."
Advent is a time of waiting—
waiting to celebrate the birth of Jesus.
In a spirit of openness to what God wants of us,
we recall our needs and the needs of all God's people.

1. For the gift of openness to God.
(*pause*)
"We are the clay, and you are our potter."
In this time of Advent,
may we be open to what God wants,
taking seriously the command to prepare

for God's coming into our lives.
Lord, hear us.

2. For the gift of faith.
(*pause*)
May we continue to grow in faith
in our God who is with us.
May we be alert to the signs of the times,
steady and blameless in our lives
as we wait for the Day of the Lord.
Lord, hear us.

3. For the gift of patience.
(*pause*)
Like the servants in the gospel story,
may we be alert and prepared,
waiting for the return of Jesus our Master.
May we be ready to greet him when he comes,
worthy of his confidence in us.
Lord, hear us.

4. For the gift of hope.
(*pause*)
Jesus commands us to be on our guard
at every hour of the day.
May we so live according to the gospel
that we may be filled with hope
as we wait for the Lord's coming.
Lord, hear us.

Priest/Leader

Creator God,
you command us to pray for the coming of
    your reign.
Help us to prepare for your coming in our lives
and to look for it with confidence and love.
We ask this through Christ our Lord. Amen.

ADVENT 2   YEAR B

Priest/Leader

"Prepare the way of the Lord."
Prepare to let God come into our lives.
Prepare to be changed by what God demands of us.
Moved by the preaching of the Baptist,
we recall our needs before God.

1. For the gift of consolation.
(pause)
God promises consolation and peace
to those who follow the way of the Lord.
In this time of Advent,
may we turn to the Lord in prayer and penance
and be filled with the peace that only God
         can give.
Lord, hear us.

2. For the gift of hope.
(pause)
We pray for the gift of hope,
confident that our God
who led us through exile and bitterness
will be our consolation,
bringing us refreshment and new hope.
Lord, hear us.

3. For the gift of repentance.
(pause)
May we be aware of our need for repentance,
regretting the evil we do to others
and resolving in this time of preparation
that sin will not control our lives
nor selfishness the values we live by.
Lord, hear us.

4. For prophets in our church.
(pause)
John the Baptist is God's messenger
who prepares the way of the Lord.
May we welcome prophets in our church
who remind us of gospel values,
making straight the paths of our God.
Lord, hear us.

Priest/Leader

In this time of waiting,
we commend ourselves and our needs
to our God who cares for us
like shepherds caring for their lambs.
We ask this through Christ our Lord.
         Amen.

Priest/Leader

"Make straight the way of the Lord."
We have listened to God's word
broken for us.
In a spirit of joy,
we bring our needs before our God.

1. For patience and joy in God's service.
(pause)
May we experience God's gifts of patience and joy,
consolation and forgiveness;
and may we live with concern for others
so that broken hearts may be bound up
and the poor cared for.
Lord, hear us.

2. For the gift of peace.
(pause)
May the God of peace make us perfect and holy
and may we be so renewed in this time of Advent
that we may be eager for the Lord's coming,
praying constantly
and holding to what is good.
Lord, hear us.

3. For a desire to be witnesses to Christ.
(pause)
Like John the Baptist, may we be witnesses
to the light of Christ,
pointing to the One who stands among us:
Jesus the Christ, sent by God
to bring us peace and joy.
Lord, hear us.

4. For the gift of being on fire for God.
(pause)
With John the Baptist as our model,
and moved by his enthusiasm for God's promises,
may we be people on fire for God's truth
filled with the Holy Spirit
and eager to live as the people of God.
Lord, hear us.

Priest/Leader

Creator God,
we rejoice in this time of Advent,
believing in your abiding love,
and looking for your day of consolation.
Grant what we need
through Christ our Lord. Amen.

ADVENT 4   YEAR B

Priest/Leader

"Do not be afraid."
As we prepare for the Day of the Lord,
we turn again to our God
whose love we acknowledge
and who is faithful to the promises.

1. For the gift of knowing God's will.
(pause)
Like David, may we be open to God's will for us.
May we not seek to impose our human desires
      on God
but be aware that God has plans
for the church and the world
that are beyond our imaginings.
Lord, hear us.

2. For the grace to be ready for Christmas.
(pause)
In these days before Christmas,
may we enter more deeply
into the hidden mysteries of God,
praying for the gift of wisdom
to live according to the gospel.
Lord, hear us.

3. For a spirit of wonder.
(pause)
Mary was troubled and confused
by the message of the angel.
Like her, may we be open to God's purposes
and may we be ready to accept God's will
in a spirit of obedience and wonder.
Lord, hear us.

4. For joy in celebrating God's good news.
(pause)

May we be filled with joy in this time of Advent
and moved by God's generosity.
May we live lives
that so reflect gospel teaching
that others may come to share our faith and joy.
Lord, hear us.

Priest/Leader

God of the promises,
lift up our hearts
as we prepare for the birth of the Messiah.
We commend our needs to you
and the needs of all the world
through Christ our Lord. Amen.

ADVENT 1   YEAR C

Priest/Leader

"Be alert at all times."
God's word has been broken for us
at the beginning of Advent.
In a spirit of openness to what God wants,
we recall our needs before the Lord.

1. For honesty and integrity.
(pause)
As we prepare for the coming of the Christ,
may we be a people of honesty and integrity,
alert to the signs of the times
as we wait for God's promises
to be fulfilled.
Lord, hear us.

2. For a desire to live as God commands.
(pause)
Paul urges us to make progress
in living as God wants.
In this time of Advent,
may we resolve to be generous in love
and blameless in God's sight.
Lord, hear us.

3. For the gift of vigilance.
(pause)
May we be alert at all times
as we wait for the Lord's coming,
faithful to the way of Christ

and praying for the strength to endure
the Day of the Lord.
Lord, hear us.

4. For hope at all times.
(*pause*)
May we be a people of hope,
confessing our God as Creator and Lord,
ready to welcome the Son of man
whose coming brings our liberation
from sin and death.
Lord, hear us.

Priest/Leader

Creator God,
you command us to look beyond this present world
to a time when we shall stand before you.
Help us prepare for that day
and to look for it with confidence and love.
We ask this through Christ our Lord. Amen.

ADVENT 2   YEAR C

Priest/Leader

"Prepare the way of the Lord."
We have listened to God's word
proclaimed and broken for us.
Encouraged by the message of John the Baptist,
we recall our needs before our God.

1. For the gift of repentance.
(*pause*)
Recalling God's promise of consolation,
we ask for the gift of repentance
so that, by our lives of integrity and justice,
all the world may come to know
the salvation of our God.
Lord, hear us.

2. For an increase in love.
(*pause*)
As we await the coming of Christ,
may we be filled with love for one another,
so that when Christ comes
he may find us blameless and without sin,
to the praise and glory of God.
Lord, hear us.

3. For a desire to prepare well for Christ's coming.
(*pause*)
We are commanded to prepare
the way for the Lord.
By lives that reflect the teaching of the gospel,
may we be ready to welcome Christ
and celebrate his coming among us.
Lord, hear us.

4. For a desire to spread the good news.
(*pause*)
The whole world waits for the coming of the Lord.
By the integrity of our lives
and the values we profess,
may we be faithful witnesses
of God's good news for all the earth.
Lord, hear us.

Priest/Leader

In this time of preparation,
we commend ourselves and all our needs
to the God of all consolation.
We make this prayer through Christ our Lord.
    Amen.

ADVENT 3   YEAR C

Priest/Leader

"Rejoice in the Lord always;
again I will say, Rejoice."
We have listened to God's word
and been strengthened by its message.
Now we turn to the Lord with joy,
bringing our needs and those of all the world.

1. For a renewed sense of hope in God.
(*pause*)
We acknowledge our God
as Creator of the universe.
May we be renewed in joyful hope,
confessing that God's ancient promises
are being fulfilled among us.
Lord, hear us.

2. For the gift of peace.
(*pause*)
We are assured that the Lord is near.

May that presence be for us
a source of deep peace,
encouraging us to prayer and thanksgiving
as we prepare for the Lord's coming.
Lord, hear us.

3. For a desire to do what God wants.
(*pause*)
In this time of preparation,
may we reflect on the teaching of the Baptist,
living lives of justice and truth,
generous toward one another
and eager to witness to the gospel.
Lord, hear us.

4. For the gift of being on fire for God.
(*pause*)
With John the Baptist as our model,
may we be on fire for God's truth;
and in this time of Advent
reflect what is of lasting value in life
as we prepare for the Lord's coming.
Lord, hear us.

Priest/Leader

God of the promises,
you made the world and all it contains.
Increase our faith in your love for the world
and bring us consolation.
We ask this through Christ our Lord. Amen.

ADVENT 4   YEAR C

Priest/Leader

"See, I have come to do your will."
God's word comforts us
and we rejoice in the God of the promises.
With confidence we turn to our God
for our needs and those of all the world.

1. For an acceptance of God's choices.
(*pause*)
God chose the least of the clans and tribes of Judah
as the people from whom the Messiah would come.
May we be open to the choices God makes for us

and acknowledge our God as living Lord
of the church and the world.
Lord, hear us.

2. For a desire to be God's faithful people.
(*pause*)
As we prepare to celebrate the birth of the Messiah,
may we renew our desire
to live as God's people,
living according to God's commands
and obedient to the law of Christ.
Lord, hear us.

3. For joy in the presence of the Lord.
(*pause*)
The infant John leaped in his mother's womb
when he recognized the presence of his Lord.
May we too be alert to God's teaching
and God's visitation
so that we may rejoice in the nearness of our God.
Lord, hear us.

4. For a spirit of wonder.
(*pause*)
Mary and Elizabeth were astonished
by the blessings of God.
In this time of Advent.
may we too be open to God's surprises
looking for the fulfillment of God's promises for us.
Lord, hear us.

Priest/Leader

God of the promises,
lift up our hearts as we prepare
for the birth of the Messiah;
and grant what we need
through Christ our Lord. Amen.

THE SEASON OF CHRISTMAS

CHRISTMAS

Priest/Leader

"To you is born this day…a Savior,
who is the Messiah, the Lord."
On this holy day,
we have listened with joy to God's good news.
With renewed confidence
we bring before our God
our needs and those of all the world.

1. For joy and peace at Christmas.
(pause)
Joy is God's gift to all the world.
May Christmas be for us and for all people
a time of joy and peace;
and may all the nations of the earth
rejoice at the birth of Jesus.
Lord, hear us.

2. For a renewed sense of hope in our world.
(pause)
May our celebration of the birth of Jesus
be a time for renewed hope in our world;
and may our joy and witness
bring the good news of salvation
to the whole human race.
Lord, hear us.

3. For thanksgiving at the birth of Jesus.
(pause)
Jesus is the Messiah, Christ the Lord.
May we be thankful to our God
for giving us a Savior born today,
bringing good news of peace and reconciliation
to all the people of the world.
Lord, hear us.

4. For peace in our families.
(pause)
May we experience peace in our families
at this special time;
and may the spirit of Christmas
be with our families and communities
in all the year ahead.
Lord, hear us.

Priest/Leader

Mighty God and Prince of Peace,
our hearts are filled with joy and confidence
as we make our prayers to you on this special day,
for you are Lord forever and ever. Amen.

THE HOLY FAMILY   YEAR A

Priest/Leader

"Let the word of Christ
dwell in you richly."
In this season of Christmas,
we thank our God for the gift of Jesus.
Today we open ourselves to God's word
teaching us how to live
as children of God in families of love.

1. For respect and acceptance in families.
(pause)
We pray for all members of our families.
May parents and children respect and honor one
        another
for their lives and their gifts.
May we care for our parents in time of need
and love them as the Lord loves us.
Lord, hear us.

2. For forgiveness and love in family life.
(pause)
All families are blessed by God
for forgiveness, patience, and gentleness.
May we be gentle in our families
—especially at this time of Christmas—
accepting one another as the Lord accepts us.
Lord, hear us.

3. For strength to live by the gospel.
(pause)
The Holy Family journeyed to Egypt
persecuted by those who feared the good news.
May we be strong in witnessing to the truth
and resolute in living
the message of the gospel.
Lord, hear us.

4. For an openness to God's purposes.
(pause)

Joseph received the news of God's purposes
in a dream.
May we be open to the promptings of the Spirit,
ready to respond to the call of the gospel
as faithful disciples of Jesus.
Lord, hear us.

Priest/Leader

God of the promises,
we bring before you the needs of families.
Bless our families and help us to be faithful
to the teaching of your Son.
We ask this through Christ our Lord. Amen.

THE HOLY FAMILY   YEAR B

Priest/Leader

"Christ stands forever at the right hand of God."
In this season of Christmas
we thank our God for the gift of Jesus.
Today we open ourselves to God's word
teaching us how to live
as children of God in families of love.

1. For trust in the promises of God.
(*pause*)
The scriptures teach us to trust
the purposes of God.
Like Abraham, may we grow in faith,
confident that our God
will fulfill all that has been promised.
Lord, hear us.

2. For a deep faith in God.
(*pause*)
The Letter to the Hebrews
praises the faith of our ancestor Abraham
who risked all things for God.
Like him, may we have deep faith in God,
within our families and communities.
Lord, hear us.

3. For a desire to be consecrated to God.
(*pause*)
The Holy Family obeyed the traditions of
their people,
offering sacrifice for purification before the Lord.

May we be aware that we too are a consecrated
people,
even in our families,
to the glory of all the nations.
Lord, hear us.

4. For openness to God's purposes.
(*pause*)
Jesus is declared by Simeon
a sign that will be rejected.
May we be open to God's mysterious purposes,
ready always to teach gospel values
especially in our families.
Lord, hear us.

Priest/Leader

God of the promises,
we bring the needs of families before you.
Bless our families and help us to be faithful
to the teaching of your Son.
We ask this through Christ our Lord. Amen.

THE HOLY FAMILY   YEAR C

Priest/Leader

"See what love the Father has given us."
In this season of Christmas
we thank our God for the gift of Jesus.
Today we open ourselves to God's word
teaching us how to live as children of God in families
of love.

1. For a willingness to belong to God.
(*pause*)
Samuel was dedicated to the Lord
even as a child.
May we always be a people of faith
knowing that we too belong to God
throughout all of life.
Lord, hear us.

2. For a desire to keep God's commandments.
(*pause*)
We are God's children,
confident in the promises of our Lord.
May we grow in our desire to keep God's
commandments

that we may live in God
as God lives in us.
Lord, hear us.

3. For an openness to God's wisdom.
(*pause*)
Jesus was found among the teachers,
discussing with them the revelation of God.
May we too be given the gift of wisdom
to help us discern God's purposes for us
in our families and communities.
Lord, hear us.

4. For the grace to live in love.
(*pause*)
Jesus lived in peace with his family,
growing in grace before God.
May our families be places of peace
where we live in mutual love and respect
for one another.
Lord, hear us.

Priest/Leader

God of the promises,
we bring the needs of families before you.
Bless our families and help us to be faithful
to the teaching of your Son.
We ask this through Christ our Lord. Amen.

MARY, MOTHER OF GOD   JANUARY 1

Priest/Leader

On this festival of Mary, Mother of God,
we have listened to God's word
and been nourished by its teaching.
With Mary as our example,
we turn to the Lord in prayer.

1. For a true devotion to Mary, Mother of God.
(*pause*)
Mary is the instrument of God's blessing
on all the people of the earth.
May we learn from her example,
discerning what God wants for us
by lives of gentleness, prayer, and service.
Lord, hear us.

2. For the gift of being thankful.
(*pause*)
May we be aware of God's blessings in our lives
and, with Mary as our mother,
thank God for the gift of the Son
born at the appointed time
to be our Savior and our brother.
Lord, hear us.

3. For a delight in God's choices.
(*pause*)
The shepherds rejoiced at the birth of the Savior
and praised God for what happened at Bethlehem.
May we too be filled with joy
that God chooses those whom society rejects
to be the bearers of good news.
Lord, hear us.

4. For an openness toward God.
(*pause*)
Mary said yes to God
when the angel asked her to be mother of the
     Messiah.
May we be open to God's promptings in life,
treasuring them in our hearts
and discerning their purpose for our lives.
Lord, hear us.

Priest/Leader

God of all consolation,
we honor Mary, mother of the Savior and
     our mother.
Listen to our prayers, for we make them
in the name of her Son, Jesus Christ our Lord.
     Amen.

EPIPHANY OF THE LORD

Priest/Leader

"When they saw that the star had stopped,
they were overwhelmed with joy."
We have listened with joy to God's word broken
     for us.
Now we approach the Lord of the universe
for our needs and those of all the world.

1. For peace in our world.
(pause)
May all the nations of the world
receive the light that God sends,
singing the praises of the Lord;
and may they work for peace in our time—
peace that is the gift of our God.
Lord, hear us.

2. For a deeper understanding of God's
        loving-kindness.
(pause)
We rejoice that God's promises have been fulfilled
among all the peoples of our world.
May we be generous in spirit to all people
and by our witness to gospel values
bring all people to acknowledge the mysteries
        of God.
Lord, hear us.

3. For the Jewish people.
(pause)
May the people of Israel be faithful
to their ancient covenant with God;
and may we who share God's blessing with them
honor the Jewish people
who were first to believe God's good news.
Lord, hear us.

4. For a sense of delight in God's presence.
(pause)
May we who celebrate this day
experience joy and delight in the presence of
        our king,
and by the honesty and integrity of our lives
be generous in sharing the gifts we have received
as faithful disciples of the Lord we worship.
Lord, hear us.

Priest/Leader

God of the universe,
your good news is for all the peoples of the earth.
Hear our prayers this day and grant what we need
through Christ our Lord. Amen.

BAPTISM OF THE LORD   YEAR A

Priest/Leader

"This is my Son, the Beloved,
with whom I am well pleased."
God's word has been proclaimed for us
on this celebration of the Lord's baptism.
Its teaching strengthens our hope in our God
as we recall our needs for the church and
        the community.

1. For a desire to be of service.
(pause)
Baptism is a call to service.
May we be good servants of the Lord,
the people of God's holy covenant
who live for justice and peace in society,
looking for ways to be of service.
Lord, hear us.

2. For tolerance in society.
(pause)
The message of the scripture
is that God has no favorites.
May we learn from this teaching
to accept and love one another
as God first loved us.
Lord, hear us.

3. For a desire to take the gospel seriously.
(pause)
May the baptism of Jesus
recall to us our own baptism
when we choose to become followers of his way,
living the gospel
by what we proclaim and what we value.
Lord, hear us.

4. For an openness to what God wants.
(pause)
John the Baptist longed
for the coming of God's chosen one.
May we be open to God's call made to us in
        our baptism;
and may we respond with faithfulness
to what God requires of us.
Lord, hear us.

Priest/Leader

God of the promises,
we rejoice in the baptism of your Son.
Make us eager to follow his way
and grant what we need
through Christ our Lord. Amen.

BAPTISM OF THE LORD YEAR B

Priest/Leader

"You are my Son, the Beloved;
with you I am well pleased."
God's word has been proclaimed for us
on this celebration of the Lord's baptism.
Its teaching strengthens our hope in our God
as we recall our needs for the church and
        the community.

1. For a desire to be faithful witnesses.
(pause)
God comforts the people,
inviting us to be witnesses to the nations.
May we be faithful in our discipleship
turning from sin in our lives
to our God who is rich in mercy.
Lord, hear us.

2. For a desire to live as God's children.
(pause)
We are God's children,
chosen by God to keep the commandments.
May we live always as God's children
confessing Jesus as the Messiah of God
and witnessing to faith in our lives.
Lord, hear us.

3. For a desire to take the gospel seriously.
(pause)
In his baptism, Jesus is declared God's Beloved.
May this celebration recall our own baptism
when we choose to become followers of his way,
living the gospel
by what we proclaim and what we value.
Lord, hear us.

4. For an openness to what God wants.
(pause)

John the Baptist longed
for the coming of God's chosen one.
May we be open to God's call made to us in
        our baptism;
and may we respond with faithfulness
to what God requires of us.
Lord, hear us.

Priest/Leader

God of the promises,
we rejoice in the baptism of your Son.
Make us eager to follow his way
and grant what we need
through Christ our Lord. Amen.

BAPTISM OF THE LORD YEAR C

Priest/Leader

"You are my Son, the Beloved;
with you I am well pleased."
God's word has been proclaimed for us
on this celebration of the Lord's baptism.
Its teaching strengthens our hope in our God
as we recall our needs for the church and
        the community.

1. For a desire to be God's messengers.
(pause)
Isaiah teaches us the consolation of God,
calling on the people to prepare for the
        Lord's coming.
May our lives proclaim the constant presence of
        our God
who gathers and cares for us
as shepherds care for their flocks.
Lord, hear us.

2. For joy in God's kindness.
(pause)
The scripture reminds us of the kindness
and love of our God for us.
May we who share Christ's baptism
be generous in our love for others
with no ambition but to do good.
Lord, hear us.

3. For a desire to take the gospel seriously.
(*pause*)
In his baptism, Jesus is declared God's Beloved.
May this celebration of his baptism
recall for us our own baptism
when we choose to become followers of his way,
by what we proclaim and what we value.
Lord, hear us.

4. For an openness to what God wants.
(*pause*)
John the Baptist longed
for the coming of God's chosen one.

May we be open to God's call made to us in
    our baptism;
and may we respond with faithfulness
to what God requires of us.
Lord, hear us.

Priest/Leader

God of the promises,
we rejoice in the baptism of your Son.
Make us eager to follow his way
and grant what we need
through Christ our Lord. Amen.

THE SEASON OF LENT

ASH WEDNESDAY

Priest/Leader

"Repent, and believe in the good news."
This is God's word to us today.
We have listened to that word
and we turn to our God in prayer.

1. For the grace of repentance in Lent.
(pause)
As we begin our forty days of Lent,
we ask God to raise in our minds
an awareness of sin in our lives
and a deep desire
to turn to our God.
Lord, hear us.

2. For a desire to be ambassadors for Christ.
(pause)
Paul teaches that we are to be Christ's ambassadors.
At this time of Lent,
may we renew our desire
to witness to the good news of God's love
revealed to us in Christ.
Lord, hear us.

3. For the grace to grow in prayer.
(pause)
We ask for a spirit of honesty before God
that we might relish the time spent in prayer,
not regarding it as a burden
but a time of joy and reflection
in the presence of our God.
Lord, hear us.

4. For a true spirit of penance during Lent.
(pause)
May we learn to follow the teaching of Jesus
and discipline ourselves during Lent
by prayer and fasting and acts of charity
so that we may have a true understanding
of what is of lasting value in life.
Lord, hear us.

Priest/Leader

Creator God,
our bodies have been marked today
with the ashes of repentance.

Listen to the prayers we have made
and, in your love, grant what we need
through Christ our Lord. Amen.

LENT 1   YEAR A

Priest/Leader

"Worship the Lord your God,
and serve only him."
In this time of Lent,
God's word commands repentance
and change of heart.
Strengthened by its teaching
we ask our God for what we need.

1. For a desire not to be ruled by evil.
(pause)
By Adam's sin, evil has entered the world
and threatens to dominate the earth.
By God's grace, may we not be ruled by sin
but resist its temptation to control our lives
by serving God alone.
Lord, hear us.

2. For a deeper appreciation of the mission of Jesus.
(pause)
May we deepen our understanding
of what God has done for us in Christ,
and by a renewed desire to follow his way
overcome evil in the world
by lives of justice, integrity, and truth.
Lord, hear us.

3. For a desire to grow in the love of God.
(pause)
In this time of Lent, may we grow closer to
    our God
by time spent in prayer and fasting.
May we follow the example of Jesus,
who found time to be alone
with the God who gives meaning to life.
Lord, hear us.

4. For an understanding of what is important in life.
(pause)
Jesus was tempted in the desert
to question the purposes of God.
By our obedience to the teaching of the Lord,

may we deepen our appreciation and understanding
of what is of ultimate value in life.
Lord, hear us.

Priest/Leader

God of all consolation,
you comforted your Son in his temptation.
Strengthen us in our resolve
to follow him faithfully.
We ask this through Christ our Lord. Amen.

LENT 2   YEAR A

Priest/Leader

"This is my Son, the Beloved…listen to him."
We have heard God's word
and been nourished by its teaching.
We now reflect on what we need in our faith journey
and present our needs to our God.

1. For faith to live as God wants.
(*pause*)
Abraham left his country and all that was familiar
to go to the land promised by God.
May we grow in faith each day
trusting in God's goodness
and God's purposes for our lives.
Lord, hear us.

2. For faith in time of doubt.
(*pause*)
Paul commands us to rely on God's power
in time of trouble.
May the transfiguration renew our faith in God's
        promises
and give us courage to believe the good news
revealed to us in Christ Jesus.
Lord, hear us.

3. For faith in Jesus, Son of God.
(*pause*)
Jesus is God's Son, the beloved.
May we be open to his word in this time of Lent,
listening to his teaching
and eager to renew our confidence
in the one who enjoys God's favor.
Lord, hear us.

4. For faith in God's kindness.
(*pause*)
Jesus commands us: "Do not be afraid."
May we grow in understanding God's goodness
        and kindness
and may we overcome fear in our lives,
recalling the resurrection of God's Son
and his triumph over evil and death.
Lord, hear us.

Priest/Leader

God of our ancestors,
you are faithful in every age.
Grant what we need to be your faithful people
through Christ our Lord. Amen.

LENT 3   YEAR A

Priest/Leader

"My food is to do the will of him who
        sent me."
The words of Jesus comfort us and challenge us.
Nourished by the teaching we have heard,
we turn to our God for what we need.

1. For a deepening of our faith in God.
(*pause*)
God cared for the people of Israel,
providing water for them
even when they complained.
May we grow in faith in the God who loves us
and who provides for us in all of life.
Lord, hear us.

2. For a desire to be at peace with God.
(*pause*)
Through the work of Christ,
we are judged righteous and at peace with God.
May this sense of peace fill us with confidence
        during Lent
as we recall God's love
poured into our hearts.
Lord, hear us.

3. For a sense of urgency in living the gospel.
(*pause*)
Jesus reached out to the Samaritan woman

and longed for her to acknowledge the truth
    about God.
By our lives of faithfulness to his teaching,
may people everywhere come to accept Jesus
as the Christ of God.
Lord, hear us.

4. For an acceptance of all people.
(pause)
Jesus spoke with the Samaritan woman,
overcoming barriers of hatred and exclusion.
May we be accepting of all people,
faithful to Jesus' command
to love one another as God loves us.
Lord, hear us.

Priest/Leader

God of the promises,
you are the God of all nations.
Teach us to be tolerant,
open, and faithful to your way.
And grant what we need
through Christ our Lord. Amen.

LENT 4   YEAR A

Priest/Leader

"The LORD is my shepherd, I shall not want."
Encouraged by this teaching
and strengthened by God's word,
we reflect on what we need
in the church and in the community.

1. For the gift to understand God's ways.
(pause)
God's ways are not our ways
and God's choices are not what we expect.
May we be alert to the God of surprises
and open to God's purposes
for the church and for the world.
Lord, hear us.

2. For the gift to live as children of the light.
(pause)
God commands us to live by the light of the gospel,
overcoming darkness and sin in our lives.
In this time of Lent,

may we resolve to walk in the light of Christ
by our faithfulness to his teaching.
Lord, hear us.

3. For the gift to see what God wants.
(pause)
Jesus is the light of the world
and his teaching is our guide in life.
May we grow in understanding his way,
living as God wants
according to God's law.
Lord, hear us.

4. For the gift of perseverance.
(pause)
The man born blind was rejected by his companions
for professing faith in Jesus the Christ.
May we persevere in faith,
professing the good news
and living by its teaching.
Lord, hear us.

Priest/Leader

God of mercy,
take pity on us
and strengthen our faith.
Grant what we need
through Christ our Lord. Amen.

LENT 5   YEAR A

Priest/Leader

"Everyone who lives and believes in me
will never die."
This teaching of the Lord
encourages us and strengthens us in life.
Nourished by God's word,
we ask our God for what we need.

1. For an openness to God's Spirit.
(pause)
It is God's Spirit that gives life.
May we be open to God at work in our lives;
and by overcoming sin and death
in what we do and what we choose
may God be glorified and God's purposes fulfilled.
Lord, hear us.

2. For a desire to be possessed by God's Spirit.
(*pause*)
May we be faithful to God's way
and to the teaching of the gospel
that God's Spirit may possess us entirely,
enabling us to be faithful witnesses,
pleasing to God.
Lord, hear us.

3. For faith in Jesus the giver of life.
(*pause*)
Jesus raised Lazarus to life,
breaking the bonds of death and setting him free.
By our faith in Jesus and his teaching,
may we be free from sin and selfishness,
living as God wants in the church and in
        the community.
Lord, hear us.

4. For a desire to witness to the Lord.
(*pause*)
Martha and Mary confessed their faith in Jesus.
Like them, may we acknowledge him
as the Lord of life,
and with confidence in his love
commend ourselves and those we love to his care.
Lord, hear us.

Priest/Leader

God of compassion,
you care for all your children.
Fill us with confidence in your power to
        save us
and grant what we need
through Christ our Lord. Amen.

LENT 1   YEAR B

Priest/Leader

"The time is fulfilled,
and the Kingdom of God has come near."
Strengthened by God's word
we turn to our Creator
for courage and perseverance in our observance
        of Lent.

1. For an understanding of God's covenant with
        the world.
(*pause*)
Recalling God's covenant with Noah
and the promise made to the world
through the sign of the rainbow,
may we grow in our understanding
of God's love for the world and all its people.
Lord, hear us.

2. For a desire to live by the gospel.
(*pause*)
Noah was saved by water
and we too are reborn in the waters
        of baptism.
May our observance of Lent
renew in us our baptismal commitment
to live by the gospel of Jesus.
Lord, hear us.

3. For a desire to resist temptation in life.
(*pause*)
Jesus was tempted
to abandon the life God had chosen
        for him.
May we resist sin in our lives
and by lives of integrity and justice
proclaim the good news from God.
Lord, hear us.

4. For an eagerness to proclaim the gospel.
(*pause*)
May we be alert to the signs of the times,
looking for ways to proclaim
the message of God's reign to all the world
by lives that are faithful to God's teaching
and values that reflect God's word.
Lord, hear us.

Priest/Leader

God of all consolation,
you sent your angels to comfort Jesus
and strengthen his desire to do your will.
Help us to be faithful followers of his teaching;
and grant what we need through Christ our Lord.
        Amen.

LENT 2 YEAR B

Priest/Leader

"If God is for us,
who is against us?"
Strengthened by God's word,
we turn to the Lord,
for all our needs.

1. For courage to be people of faith.
(*pause*)
Abraham is our father in faith.
May his desire to obey God
strengthen us in this time of Lent
to new resolutions of trust
in God's faithfulness and love.
Lord, hear us.

2. For a spirit of thanks to God.
(*pause*)
May we grow in understanding
God's gifts to the church and to the world;
and in this time of Lent
give thanks for the gift of Jesus
who pleads for us before our God.
Lord, hear us.

3. For renewal in our commitment to the
        way of Jesus.
(*pause*)
In the tradition of Moses and Elijah,
Jesus is both teacher and prophet.
Following God's command,
may we learn to listen to the beloved Son
that, like him, our lives may be transformed
        by God.
Lord, hear us.

4. For delight in the presence of God.
(*pause*)
Like Peter, James, and John,
may we be filled with delight
in the presence of God in our lives;
and may we be renewed in our desire
to live as disciples of God's Son.
Lord, hear us.

Priest/Leader

God of the transfiguration,
fill us with your love and comfort.
Make us eager to listen to your Son,
even to death and resurrection.
We ask this through Christ our Lord.
        Amen.

LENT 3 YEAR B

Priest/Leader

"The law of the LORD is perfect,
reviving the soul."
We have shared God's word
and reflected on its message.
We now ask our God
for what we need to be faithful to
        that teaching.

1. For a deeper understanding of God's law.
(*pause*)
May we receive the gift of wisdom
to understand God's law and God's way,
not simply as revealed to a people long ago
but given to us to live out
in our time.
Lord, hear us.

2. For faith in God's promises.
(*pause*)
We preach Christ crucified,
according to the mysterious purposes of God.
May we have faith in God's foolishness
that is greater than our wisdom,
and accept the cross with humility and hope.
Lord, hear us.

3. For an awareness of God's grace.
(*pause*)
May we learn from the example of Jesus
that God's love cannot be purchased
but is given to those
who constantly seek
to do God's will.
Lord, hear us.

4. For renewal of zeal among God's people.
(*pause*)
May we be constant in living as God's people
in the church and in the community.
May we be faithful in our concerns
for God's teaching and God's truth,
zealous witnesses to the way of Christ.
Lord, hear us.

Priest/Leader

God of all compassion,
fill us with zeal for your teaching
that people everywhere may come to know you
and live as you would have them live.
We ask this through Christ our Lord. Amen.

LENT 4   YEAR B

Priest/Leader

"For God so loved the world
that he gave his only Son."
On our journey through Lent,
we bring before the Lord
our fears, our hopes,
our concerns, and our needs.

1. For a deeper faith in God's activity in the world.
(*pause*)
God inspired Cyrus, king of Persia,
to console the Jewish people
in their time of exile.
May we renew our faith
in God's saving presence in our world.
Lord, hear us.

2. For a greater awareness of God's generous love.
(*pause*)
We hope in God because God is faithful
and we trust in God's generous love
that has saved us, in Christ.
May we show forth God's goodness
in how we live and what we value.
Lord, hear us.

3. For a spirit of self-giving.
(*pause*)
Jesus gave himself for all of us

when he was lifted up on the cross.
May we share his spirit of self-giving,
overcoming the darkness of greed
by the light of our concern.
Lord, hear us.

4. For an eagerness to walk in the light.
(*pause*)
May we be a people who walk in the light of Christ,
avoiding the darkness of sin and death;
and may we grow in faith in Jesus,
filled with the light that comes from God
and living by the truth revealed in Christ.
Lord, hear us.

Priest/Leader

God of light,
you command us to choose light over darkness.
Help us to overcome sin in our lives
to live by the truth of the gospel.
We ask this through Christ our Lord. Amen.

LENT 5   YEAR B

Priest/Leader

"And I, when I am lifted up from the earth,
will draw all people to myself."
God's word has been broken for us
and we have reflected on its teaching.
Now we bring before God our needs
and those of all God's people.

1. For a desire to live as God wants.
(*pause*)
"I will be their God, and they shall be my people."
May the new covenant that God has written on our
       hearts
increase our desire to live as God wants
by the commandments planted deeply within us.
Lord, hear us.

2. For a deeper understanding of God's purposes.
(*pause*)
Jesus learned obedience through suffering
and became the source of salvation for all.
May we grow in accepting
the mysterious purposes of God

who brings resurrection out of suffering and death.
Lord, hear us.

3. For a rich harvest among God's people.
(pause)
We believe that the death of a single grain
    of wheat
can yield a rich harvest.
May we so die to self and live for others
that the world may turn from selfishness
and enjoy a harvest of peace and justice.
Lord, hear us.

4. For a spirit of service.
(pause)
May we be worthy disciples of Jesus,
looking for ways to be of service
in the community and in the church,
responding to those in need as the Lord showed
in his life and his death.
Lord, hear us.

Priest/Leader

God of love and service,
your Son died to bring a rich harvest of life
    for others.
Awaken in us a desire to be servants like him,
faithful to the covenant you have written in our
    hearts.
We ask this through Christ our Lord. Amen.

LENT 1   YEAR C

Priest/Leader

"One does not live by bread alone."
As we begin our journey through Lent,
scripture reminds us of what is important in life.
Nourished by God's word,
we reflect on what we need
to live as God wants.

1. For a deeper faith in God.
(pause)
We belong to a covenant people
that has always trusted in God's promises.
As we begin our Lenten journey,
may it be for us a time of reflection

on God's saving deeds throughout our history.
Lord, hear us.

2. For an increase in prayer.
(pause)
In this time of Lent,
may God's word be on our lips and in
    our hearts.
May we confess Jesus as Lord,
calling on his name
to make us righteous in God's sight.
Lord, hear us.

3. For a sense of what is important in life.
(pause)
Jesus was tempted to turn from God's way
and be ruled by other values in life.
May we be his faithful followers,
leading lives that are sustained
by gospel teaching about integrity and truth.
Lord, hear us.

4. For the strength to resist evil.
(pause)
By God's grace, Jesus resisted evil in his life.
May we too call on God in time of trouble
and be moved to choose what God wants,
rejecting the attraction of sin
and refusing to be ruled by its power.
Lord, hear us.

Priest/Leader

God of our ancestors,
we are the people of your covenant,
the sisters and brothers of Jesus.
Listen to our prayers; for we make them
through Christ our Lord. Amen.

LENT 2   YEAR C

Priest/Leader

"This is my Son, my Chosen."
In this time of Lent,
we are strengthened on our journey
by the transfiguration of Jesus.
Nourished by God's word
we recall our needs before the Lord.

1. For renewed faith in our God.
(*pause*)
Abraham is our father in faith
because he believed in the promises of God.
May we too be faithful to our covenant
        with God,
putting our trust in God's love,
seeking always to do what God wants.
Lord, hear us.

2. For a desire to follow the law of Christ.
(*pause*)
Like St. Paul, may we follow the rule of life,
eager to live as Jesus commands;
and by our prayers and fasting during Lent,
may we honor the cross of Christ,
imitating the one who died that we might
        have life.
Lord, hear us.

3. For a delight in the presence of our God.
(*pause*)
Peter, James, and John were filled with joy
in the presence of God.
May we too be joyful in the Lord,
seeking God's company in prayer and reflection,
listening to the teaching about how we are to live.
Lord, hear us.

4. For a sense of wonder at the transfiguration
        of Jesus.
(*pause*)
Like the apostles on the mountain
who witnessed the transfiguration of Jesus,
may we be filled with wonder
in the presence and witness of God's holy ones
and with a deep desire to listen to God's
        chosen Son.
Lord, hear us.

Priest/Leader

God of the transfiguration,
fill us with delight in your presence,
and grant what we need
through Christ our Lord.
        Amen.

Priest/Leader

"Unless you repent, you will all perish."
God's powerful word teaches us
to turn from sin.
In a spirit of sincere repentance,
we ask the Lord
for what we need.

1. For an awareness of God's holiness.
(*pause*)
Moses stood on holy ground
and was afraid to look at his God.
May we be aware of God's holiness
and be filled with a sense of wonder
at what God has done for the people.
Lord, hear us.

2. For a desire to please God.
(*pause*)
May we be filled with a desire to please God
        in life,
aware of the power of sin
and fearful of how it can control us;
and may we repent of those things
that turn us from God's ways.
Lord, hear us.

3. For reconciliation with God and with
        one another.
(*pause*)
In this time of Lent,
may we seek reconciliation
with God and with one another;
and by our prayer and fasting
be renewed in our desire to live as God wants.
Lord, hear us.

4. For a spirit of obedience to God.
(*pause*)
May we seek to obey God's will,
acknowledging our God as Lord of the universe
whose ways are not our ways
and who commands us to bear fruit
in how we live and what we value.
Lord, hear us.

Priest/Leader

God of the universe,
you are faithful to the promises.
Listen to our prayers for what we need
through Christ our Lord. Amen.

| LENT 4 | YEAR C |

Priest/Leader

"This son of mine was dead and is alive again;
he was lost and is found."
In our journey through Lent,
scripture reminds us of God's power to save.
Strengthened by that teaching,
we turn to our God for what we need.

1. For a spirit of thanksgiving.
(pause)
Like the ancient people of Israel,
may we rejoice that the Lord has rescued us
from slavery to sin and death;
and may we celebrate God's love
by lives of faithfulness and trust.
Lord, hear us.

2. For a desire to be ambassadors for Christ.
(pause)
Paul teaches us that we are ambassadors for Christ,
who reconciled us to God.
May we be good stewards of our Master,
proclaiming his message in our daily lives
and living the reconciliation promised by God.
Lord, hear us.

3. For an appreciation of God's tender mercy.
(pause)
The parables of Jesus
teach us about God's merciful love.
May we deepen our understanding of God's care
and the lengths to which God goes
to show us love and mercy.
Lord, hear us.

4. For generosity toward others.
(pause)
The father welcomed his wayward child—
a sign of God's generosity and love.

May we be generous toward others,
willing to forget past sins
and to welcome others as God welcomes us.
Lord, hear us.

Priest/Leader

God of love,
you have reconciled us to yourself and made
         us your children.
Listen to our prayers
and grant what we need
through Christ our Lord. Amen.

| LENT 5 | YEAR C |

Priest/Leader

"Neither do I condemn you."
Jesus' words to the woman in the gospel
bring comfort to all who follow his way.
Strengthened by his teaching,
we reflect on what we need
for the church and for the world.

1. For thanksgiving to God for forgiveness.
(pause)
May we be a people who know we are forgiven,
aware of God's love for each of us,
beginning again in every generation;
and may we be a people of thanksgiving
for God's generous gifts to us.
Lord, hear us.

2. For a desire to serve in the community.
(pause)
Like Paul, we race for the prize God has promised.
Like him, may we desire to be of service to others
in the church and in the community
so that we may reach the perfection
that comes from God.
Lord, hear us.

3. For a spirit of compassion.
(pause)
Jesus accepted the woman in the gospel
with kindness and mercy.
May we be faithful followers of Jesus,
careful not to condemn others,

witnessing to the compassion of our Lord.
Lord, hear us.

4. For the grace to avoid hypocrisy.
(pause)
The rulers of the people
showed their hypocrisy
when confronted by Jesus.
May we be people of the truth

witnessing to the gospel by lives of integrity.
Lord, hear us.

Priest/Leader

God of compassion and love,
teach us your ways.
Hear the prayers we make
through Christ our Lord. Amen.

HOLY WEEK

PASSION/PALM SUNDAY

Priest/Leader

We have begun our Holy Week observances.
We have celebrated Jesus' entry to Jerusalem
and watched the mood change from joy
      to sadness.
Yet in hope, we present our needs before our God.

1. For Christian people everywhere.
(pause)
At the beginning of this Holy Week,
we pray for all our Christian brothers and sisters
that we may follow the example of Jesus,
who emptied himself for us
that we might learn to be of service to all.
Lord, hear us.

2. For those who suffer for what they believe.
(pause)
We pray for those in our world
who, like Jesus, are unjustly persecuted.
By our prayers and actions,
may we be in solidarity with those
who suffer for justice and truth.
Lord, hear us.

3. For a sense of peace in the midst of suffering.
(pause)
May we be granted the gift of inner peace
when we experience pain at the hands of others.
And may Christians everywhere
support those who are suffering
by our prayers and understanding and love.
Lord, hear us.

4. For a fruitful observance of Holy Week.
(pause)
May we use this Holy Week profitably
—for reflection and prayer
—for renewal and repentance
—for acts of charity
—for worship and sharing.
Lord, hear us.

Priest/Leader

God of compassion, keep us faithful
even in times of suffering;

and bring us to Easter joy.
We ask this through Christ our Lord. Amen.

HOLY THURSDAY

Priest/Leader

On this holy night,
we remember with joy the Supper of the Lord.
Gathered as God's people
and nourished by the breaking of God's word,
we recall our needs and the needs of the church.

1. For a spirit of service.
(pause)
Jesus the Master washed the feet
of his followers.
May we learn from him that God's way
demands our service of others
in the community and in the church.
Lord, hear us.

2. For those called to ministry in the churches.
(pause)
May all who are called to ministry in the churches
be wise leaders in the community,
eager to share God's word
with their fellow servants
in the church.
Lord, hear us.

3. For renewal in our following of Jesus.
(pause)
Jesus gave us a new commandment:
to love one another as he loved us.
May we deepen our desire to live that
      commandment
that people everywhere may recognize us
as followers of Christ.
Lord, hear us.

4. For a desire to be broken for others.
(pause)
May the broken bread
and the outpoured wine
be symbols of God's people
willing to be broken and poured out
for the service of the world.
Lord, hear us.

Priest/Leader

Ruler of the universe, God most high,
we thank you for the gift of your Son.
Give us the strength we need
to be his faithful followers.
We ask this through Christ our Lord. Amen.

GENERAL INTERCESSIONS FOR GOOD FRIDAY

1. For the church.

Let us pray for God's church throughout the world.
(pause)
Lord, guide your church throughout the world.
May the church proclaim your good news
and bring your salvation to all people.
We ask this through Christ our Lord. Amen.

2. For the pope and all leaders in the churches.

Let us pray for the leaders of God's people.
(pause)
Lord, guide the pope
and all the leaders in the churches.
May their preaching and their example
help us grow in love
and become more faithful followers of your Son.
We ask this through Christ our Lord. Amen.

3. For all members of our churches.

Let us pray for all who belong to the people of God.
(pause)
Lord, your Spirit guides the church
and makes it holy.
Help us to be faithful witnesses
to the way of Jesus
in what we do and what we proclaim.
We ask this through Christ our Lord. Amen.

4. For those preparing for baptism.

Let us pray for those who are preparing for baptism.
(pause)
Lord, you constantly bless your church
with new members.

Increase the faith and understanding of those
preparing for baptism at this time.
We ask this through Christ our Lord. Amen.

5. For unity among Christians.

Let us pray for Christian unity.
(pause)
Lord, look with favor on all
who follow the way of your Son
and share the same baptism.
Bring us all to the fullness of faith
and keep us one in the bonds of love.
We ask this through Christ our Lord. Amen.

6. For the Jewish people.

Let us pray for the Jewish people,
the first to hear God's word and share God's
    covenant.
(pause)
Lord, long ago, you gave the promises
to Abraham and to his descendants forever.
We pray for our Jewish sisters and brothers
as they strive to be faithful to your covenant with
    them.
We ask this through Christ our Lord. Amen.

7. For those who do not believe in Christ.

Let us pray for those who do not believe in Christ
that they may be shown the way to salvation.
(pause)
We pray for our sisters and brothers
who do not acknowledge Christ in their hearts.
By our witness to his teaching,
may they discover the truth about Jesus.
We ask this through Christ our Lord. Amen.

8. For those who do not believe in God.

Let us pray for those who do not believe in God
that they may find God by following what is right in
    their hearts.
(pause)
Lord, you created people to know you
and enjoy peace in your love.
May our faithfulness in reflecting your love and
    mercy

bring those who do not believe in you
to confess you as Lord and God of all.
We ask this through Christ our Lord. Amen.

9. For those in public office.

Let us pray for those who serve the community
in public office.
(pause)
Lord, in your goodness,
watch over those in public office
so that people everywhere
may know freedom, security, and peace.
We ask this through Christ our Lord. Amen.

10. For those in special need.

Let us pray for the sick, the dying,
those who suffer in war and famine,
and all who need our prayers at this time.
(pause)
Lord, give strength to the weary
and new courage to those who have lost heart.
We commend to you all who are in need
in our world and in our community.
We ask this through Christ our Lord. Amen.

THE SEASON OF EASTER

EASTER VIGIL

Priest/Leader

The Lord is risen! Heaven and earth rejoice
in the reconciliation of God with all creation.
Filled with Easter joy,
we bring to God our needs
for the church and for the world.

1. For the community that is called the church.
(pause)
We are an Easter people
and we ask God's blessing on the church.
May our witness to the resurrection
be a source of joy and hope
in a world of despair and pain.
Lord, hear us.

2. For new believers everywhere.
(pause)
May those who have been baptized this night
(especially X and X who have joined our
      community)
know the peace that only God can give.
May they always be faithful
to the baptismal promises they have made.
Lord, hear us.

3. For a deeper faith in the risen Christ.
(pause)
By the death and rising of Jesus,
sin has been destroyed
and no longer has power over us.
May we live no longer as slaves of sin
but alive for God in Christ Jesus.
Lord, hear us.

4. For the world in darkness.
(pause)
May the light of Christ
that overcame the darkness of death
so shine in our lives
that people everywhere will be comforted
by our charity and love.
Lord, hear us.

Priest/Leader

Creator God of heaven and earth,
we bless you and thank you for this holy night.
Help us be faithful witnesses to the risen Christ.
We ask this through Christ our Lord. Amen.

EASTER DAY

Priest/Leader

Christ our hope is risen. Alleluia!
In our rejoicing at the resurrection of our Savior,
we turn to our God and recall our needs
and those of all the church.

1. For the church throughout the world.
(pause)
On this Easter Day,
may Christians everywhere
experience the joy of the risen Jesus
and be renewed in faith and hope
for the forgiveness of sin.
Lord, hear us.

2. For a desire to believe the good news.
(pause)
May the triumph of Jesus over death
be a comfort to those who are in distress.
And may we who have been reborn in Christ
reject all sin in our lives
and live by sincerity and truth.
Lord, hear us.

3. For a desire to live a new life in Christ.
(pause)
May the joy of this Easter Day
encourage us to grow in Christ
so that like him
we may choose to walk in the light
and reject the darkness of sin.
Lord, hear us.

4. For a commitment to be witnesses to Christ.
(pause)
May we share the enthusiasm
of Mary Magdalene, Peter, and John
to be witnesses to the resurrection of Jesus
by our faithfulness to his teaching

and the gospel values that mark our lives.
Lord, hear us.

Priest/Leader

God of all faithfulness,
you raised Jesus to newness of life.
Send your Spirit into our hearts
that even in troubled times
we may be people of hope.
We ask this through Christ our risen Lord. Amen.

EASTER 2   YEAR A

Priest/Leader

"My Lord and my God."
With Thomas, we confess Jesus
as Lord and Christ.
Strengthened by the message of God's word,
we turn to our God
for what we need.

1. For the gift of generosity.
(*pause*)
The first Christians were generous toward one
      another,
sharing what they owned for the love of God.
May we too be people of kindness,
known for our concern for the poor and
      the helpless,
and generous in sharing what we have.
Lord, hear us.

2. For the gift of hope and joy.
(*pause*)
The resurrection of Jesus fills us with hope and joy.
May the good news of Jesus raised from the dead
comfort us in time of trouble
and remind us of God's great love
and God's saving promises.
Lord, hear us.

3. For the gift of faith.
(*pause*)
Like Thomas, may we long to see the risen Jesus.
May we grow in faith,
recognizing him in the broken bread
and the wine shared—

everlasting signs of God's presence with
      God's people.
Lord, hear us.

4. For the gift of forgiveness.
(*pause*)
Jesus commanded his followers to forgive
      one another.
May we be people of forgiveness,
accepting one another in love,
not bearing grudges
but striving to live in peace with all.
Lord, hear us.

Priest/Leader

God of life and love,
your Spirit fills us with confidence.
Listen to the prayers we make
and grant what we need
through Christ our Lord. Amen.

EASTER 3   YEAR A

Priest/Leader

"Then their eyes were opened,
and they recognized him."
As God's people, we gather
to break the bread in memory of Jesus.
Nourished by God's word, broken for us,
we commend ourselves to our God.

1. For a deeper understanding of Jesus' resurrection.
(*pause*)
In this Easter time, may we grow in faith and
      understanding
about Jesus raised from the dead.
May we acknowledge God's purposes at work in
      him—
in his life, his teaching, his death, and resurrection—
and may we be faithful in following his way.
Lord, hear us.

2. For a deeper understanding of the price of
      our salvation.
(*pause*)
God sent Jesus
to free us from sin and death.

Acknowledging that it cost the death of the
    sinless one,
may we be constant in praising God
for what has been done for us in Christ.
Lord, hear us.

3. For a deeper understanding of Christ crucified.
(*pause*)
May we seek to understand
the mysterious purposes of God,
who allowed Jesus to be crucified and to die for us.
May we be comforted by the depth of God's
    love for us
and strengthened by the good news of the
    resurrection.
Lord, hear us.

4. For a deeper understanding of Jesus present
    with us.
(*pause*)
May we grow in faith about Jesus present
    among us
and, like the disciples on the road to Emmaus,
be strengthened in life's journey
by the knowledge that Jesus is with us
especially in the breaking of the bread.
Lord, hear us.

Priest/Leader

God of the promises,
you are with us always.
Strengthen our faith in your love
and grant what we need.
We ask this through Christ our Lord. Amen.

EASTER 4   YEAR A

Priest/Leader

"I have come that they may have life,
and have it abundantly."
The good news of Jesus the shepherd
encourages us in our journey through life.
Strengthened by the teaching of the Bible,
we are confident before our God,
asking for what we need.

1. For a desire to renew our baptismal promises.
(*pause*)
Peter proclaimed Jesus as Lord and Christ.
By our baptism, we have put on Christ
and refuse to be dominated by sin.
In this Easter time, we renew that commitment,
asking God's grace to be faithful to our baptism.
Lord, hear us.

2. For a desire to understand the sufferings
    of Jesus.
(*pause*)
The sufferings of Jesus
reflect the mysterious purposes of God.
When suffering and sorrows are part of our lives,
may we strive to imitate Jesus, putting
    our trust
in God's merciful love.
Lord, hear us.

3. For a desire to follow Jesus the shepherd.
(*pause*)
May we acknowledge Jesus the shepherd,
the one who leads his people.
May we listen always to his voice,
faithful disciples of his teaching
that brings us life in its fullness.
Lord, hear us.

4. For a desire to witness to the truth.
(*pause*)
Jesus is the holy one of God,
the teacher and shepherd of all.
By lives that reflect gospel values,
may we be witnesses to the truth that
    he taught
and the fullness of life that he promised.
Lord, hear us.

Priest/Leader

God of compassion,
look on us with favor
as we seek to imitate your Son.
And grant us what we need
through Christ our Lord. Amen.

EASTER 5   YEAR A

Priest/Leader

"I am the way, and the truth, and the life."
God's holy word nourishes us by its teaching.
Filled with Easter joy, we turn to our God
for what we need in the church and in the
      community.

1. For a spirit of service to others.
(pause)
The first Christians shared all they possessed.
They chose special people for the ministry of service
as a sign of their love for one another.
May service be the mark of all our Christian lives
in the church and in the community.
Lord, hear us.

2. For a spirit of openness to God.
(pause)
Jesus is the stone rejected by others
yet chosen by God to be the keystone of God's reign.
May we recognize that we are God's consecrated
      people;
and may we be open to God's choices
for the church and for the world.
Lord, hear us.

3. For a spirit of trust in God's promises.
(pause)
Jesus commands us not to be troubled.
May our confidence in God be strengthened
and our hope confirmed
in the promises God has made
for those who follow the way of Jesus.
Lord, hear us.

4. For a spirit of truth in our lives.
(pause)
Jesus is the way, the truth, and the life.
May we be a people dedicated to the truth
about God, about the Christ,
and about God's purposes
for all the people of the world.
Lord, hear us.

Priest/Leader

God of the promises,
you have loved all your creation from
      the beginning.
Renew our hope in you
and grant what we need
through Christ our Lord. Amen.

EASTER 6   YEAR A

Priest/Leader

"I will not leave you orphaned," says the Lord.
This good news comforts us, especially in times of
      distress.
Strengthened by the teaching of the word,
we turn with confidence to our God
for what we need.

1. For a desire to witness to the gospel.
(pause)
By lives that reflect gospel teaching
and the values of the way of Jesus,
may others be attracted to believe God's word.
May they accept baptism and the gifts of God's Spirit
that bring life in all its fullness.
Lord, hear us.

2. For a desire to reverence the Lord.
(pause)
Jesus was put to death for us
and rose to bring us new life.
May we always reverence the Lord Jesus in our
      hearts,
confident in bearing witness to what we believe
about the Christ and the teaching we have received.
Lord, hear us.

3. For a desire to keep the commandments.
(pause)
May we strive always to obey the commandments of
      the Lord,
especially to love others and serve them;
and, by our care for others,
may we show forth our love for the Christ
and our faith in his teaching that brings life forever.
Lord, hear us.

4. For a desire to prepare for the coming of the Spirit.

(pause)

Jesus promised to send another Advocate,
the Spirit of truth who would be with the community.
By our witness to the truth of the gospel
and our faithfulness to the teaching of Jesus,
may we prepare well to celebrate the coming of God's Spirit.
Lord, hear us.

Priest/Leader

God of love,
you have never left us
and your Spirit guides us always.
Listen to the prayers we make
through Christ our Lord. Amen.

EASTER 7   YEAR A

Priest/Leader

"I am asking on their behalf…
because they are yours."
Nourished by God's word, broken for us,
we turn to our God with confidence
for what we need.

1. For a spirit of prayer.

(pause)

The first Christians were devoted to prayer,
acknowledging it as central for the life of faith.
May we too relish the time spent in prayer,
recalling God's goodness to us
and discerning God's purposes for our lives.
Lord, hear us.

2. For a spirit of witness.

(pause)

Jesus suffered and died
for the truth about God.
May we be strengthened by his example
when we profess what we believe
and witness to the truth about the gospel.
Lord, hear us.

3. For a spirit of perseverance in life.

(pause)

Eternal life is to know God
and the Christ whom God has sent.
May we be strong in faith and love
so that God may be glorified
in the church and in the community.
Lord, hear us.

4. For a spirit of love for one another.

(pause)

May we be so filled with love for one another
that God's name may be held holy;
and may we hold to the teaching we have received
so that the work of Jesus
may continue in our time.
Lord, hear us.

Priest/Leader

God of the promises,
your Son Jesus is the way to eternal life.
We glorify him and we glorify you.
Listen to our prayer and grant what we need
through Christ our Lord. Amen.

EASTER 2   YEAR B

Priest/Leader

"Blessed are those who have not seen
and yet have come to believe."
In our Easter celebrations,
we have listened to the word
and professed our faith.
Now we turn to God in prayer
for all our needs.

1. For charity toward others in the community.

(pause)

The first Christians practiced charity
and cared for one another.
May we too be concerned for those in our communities
who need our prayers, our time,
and our generosity.
Lord, hear us.

2. For an awareness that we are God's children.
(*pause*)
Scripture teaches us
that we are children of God.
May we be aware that we are begotten by God
and live by faith
as God commands us.
Lord, hear us.

3. For the gift of faith.
(*pause*)
Like Thomas, may we long to see the risen Jesus.
May we grow in faith,
recognizing him in the broken bread
and the wine shared—
everlasting signs of God's presence with
        God's people.
Lord, hear us.

4. For the gift of forgiveness.
(*pause*)
Jesus commanded his followers to forgive
        one another.
May we be people of forgiveness,
accepting one another in love,
not bearing grudges
but striving to live in peace with all.
Lord, hear us.

Priest/Leader

God of love,
we have died with Christ and now live with him.
May we be eager to obey the commands of God
and to forgive one another.
We ask this through Christ our Lord.
        Amen.

EASTER 3   YEAR B

Priest/Leader

"We may be sure that we know him,
if we obey his commandments."
We have listened to God's word
and with confidence we approach our God
for the needs of our communities.

1. For the joy of being witnesses to Christ.
(*pause*)
Peter teaches us to be faithful followers
        of Christ
in our daily lives.
By our witness to the teaching of the gospel,
may God's name be glorified
in the church and in the community.
Lord, hear us.

2. For a desire to keep the commandments of God.
(*pause*)
May we live always by the commandments
        of God,
revealed in the life and teaching of his Son;
and by lives that are faithful to his way
and avoiding all sin,
may we witness to the truth of God's love for
        the world.
Lord, hear us.

3. For a deeper understanding of Christ's presence
        among us.
(*pause*)
The disciples recognized Jesus
in the breaking of the bread.
May we who gather in his name
learn to acknowledge his presence among us,
giving us strength to live as he commanded.
Lord, hear us.

4. For the gift of peace.
(*pause*)
Aware of Christ's presence among us today,
may we celebrate the gift of peace
and become peacemakers
in the church and in the world,
in our families and communities.
Lord, hear us.

Priest/Leader

God of the promises,
help us to be strong in faith and hope and love,
and renewed in our desire
to live as you command,
through Christ our Lord.
        Amen.

EASTER 4   YEAR B

Priest/Leader

"I am the good shepherd."
Strengthened by God's word
and God's promises,
we recall our needs
and the needs of the church and the world.

1. For those who need our help in the
       community.
(pause)
In Jesus' name,
Peter healed the crippled man.
May we too reach out to others in need
and by our faith in Christ and his power to save
bring healing and wholeness to our
       communities.
Lord, hear us.

2. For a desire to live as children of God.
(pause)
God's love for us is so lavish
that we have become God's children.
May this understanding fill us with confidence
to face the future with hope,
helping us overcome fear and despair in life.
Lord, hear us.

3. For the leaders in the churches.
(pause)
With Jesus the good shepherd as their model,
may the leaders in the churches
be faithful in what they preach and teach
about the purposes of God
revealed in Christ.
Lord, hear us.

4. For unity in the church of God.
(pause)
Jesus prayed for unity
among those who follow the good shepherd.
May we look for ways to be one flock,
faithful disciples of the Holy One
who laid down his life for the people.
Lord, hear us.

Priest/Leader

God of love, may we be faithful
in our following of Jesus the good shepherd,
listening for his voice
and following his way.
We ask this through Christ our Lord. Amen.

EASTER 5   YEAR B

Priest/Leader

"I am the vine, you are the branches."
Strengthened by God's word,
we call to mind our needs
for ourselves and for our community.

1. For courage in being witnesses to Christ.
(pause)
Paul proclaimed his faith in Christ
boldly and without fear.
May we too be Christ's faithful witnesses
by the honesty of our actions
and our faithfulness to gospel values.
Lord, hear us.

2. For a desire to keep God's commandments.
(pause)
Our love for God is shown
by what we do and how we live.
May those who belong to the community called
       the church
be marked by a desire to be faithful
to God's commandments.
Lord, hear us.

3. For a longing to bear fruit for God.
(pause)
Jesus is the true vine.
May we grow in our desire
to live as his disciples,
imitating him in his life and teaching
and bearing abundant fruit for God.
Lord, hear us.

4. For an awareness of our closeness to Christ.
(pause)
Jesus is the vine; we are the branches.
May we learn to cherish

our closeness to Christ
so that we may share his life
and be one with him.
Lord, hear us.

Priest/Leader

God of all faithfulness,
you bless your people always.
Grant that we may be eager to do your will in all
    things
and bear fruit to your glory.
We ask this through Christ our Lord. Amen.

EASTER 6   YEAR B

Priest/Leader

"You are my friends if you do what I command you."
As friends of Jesus,
we have listened to God's word.
Now we turn to our God in prayer,
confident that we will be heard.

1. For an awareness of God's love for all people.
(*pause*)
God has no favorites,
and no nation or people can claim God as their own.
May we learn tolerance of other faiths and cultures,
acknowledging that those who seek justice and truth
are pleasing and acceptable to God.
Lord, hear us.

2. For the gift of loving one another.
(*pause*)
May we take to heart the command to love,
learning from the example of Jesus himself.
May we try to live out this command,
forgiving and accepting one another
as children of God.
Lord, hear us.

3. For a deeper understanding of God's love for us.
(*pause*)
God's love is measured by the gift of Jesus, the only
    Son
who laid down his life for his friends.
May we grow in understanding
the mystery and meaning of this great love

and respond to it by our own self-giving.
Lord, hear us.

4. For a desire to deepen our friendship with God.
(*pause*)
We are no longer servants but friends of the Lord,
chosen to bear fruit in our world.
May our friendship with our Lord deepen
    and grow,
reaching to the perfection of loving one another
that God commands.
Lord, hear us.

Priest/Leader

God of all nations,
you command us to love one another.
Increase our faith
and help us grow in love.
We ask this through Christ our Lord. Amen.

EASTER 7   YEAR B

Priest/Leader

"I have sent them into the world."
We are an Easter people,
strengthened and renewed by the word of God.
Now we bring before our God
our own needs and those of all the church.

1. For those called to be teachers and preachers in
    the church.
(*pause*)
Like Matthias, may teachers and preachers
be people of integrity and faith,
eager to witness to the good news about Jesus
and supported by the prayers and encouragement
of all who belong to God's people.
Lord, hear us.

2. For a desire to live as God commands.
(*pause*)
God's command is that we love one another.
May we take this teaching to heart
so that God may live in us
and we may share the Spirit of God's love
by what we do and what we value.
Lord, hear us.

3. For a deep faith in God's love.
(*pause*)
Jesus teaches us about God's love for each of us.
May our faith in God's love
comfort and strengthen us
when we are called to witness to the truth
in our world.
Lord, hear us.

4. For a commitment to live by the truth.
(*pause*)
May we always be true to God's name,
constant in using gospel teaching
and the example of Jesus
to resist false values
and unjust systems in our world.
Lord, hear us.

Priest/Leader

God of love, consecrate your people in truth.
Keep us true to your name.
Help us to love as you command
so that we may share your joy to the full.
We ask this through Christ our Lord. Amen.

EASTER 2   YEAR C

Priest/Leader

"Blessed are those who have not seen
and yet have come to believe."
God's word fills our hearts at this Easter time.
With confidence and joy,
we turn to the Lord for what we need
in the community and in the church.

1. For confidence in God's promises.
(*pause*)
The first Christians trusted God's promises
to add to their number each day.
May we too be confident of God's care,
and, by our concern for the sick and the outcast,
witness to God's love for all peoples.
Lord, hear us.

2. For a desire to be faithful disciples.
(*pause*)
Like John on the island of Patmos,

who was called to preach God's word
and witness to Jesus,
may we never lose hope in following the gospel
but confess our faith always in the Living One
       of God.
Lord, hear us.

3. For a spirit of forgiveness.
(*pause*)
God's gift of forgiveness has been poured out
on the community that is called the church.
May each of us be filled with the Holy Spirit,
forgiving one another
as God has forgiven us.
Lord, hear us.

4. For a spirit of peace.
(*pause*)
Jesus' gift of peace filled the disciples
and gave them new strength for their mission.
May we be filled with the peace that is given
to those who confess Jesus
as "my Lord and my God."
Lord, hear us

Priest/Leader

God, the giver of life,
fill us with your Spirit
and grant what we need
to be faithful witnesses to the resurrection.
We ask this through Christ our Lord. Amen.

EASTER 3   YEAR C

Priest/Leader

"Worthy is the Lamb that was slaughtered
to receive power and wealth and wisdom and
       might."
Filled with Easter joy, we worship the Lamb of God.
Nourished by God's word,
we turn to the Lord in prayer.

1. For the grace to witness to the resurrection.
(*pause*)
Like the apostles, may we be constant
in our witness to the resurrection;
and by our love for one another

and the teaching we profess,
may others be encouraged to believe the
        good news.
Lord, hear us.

2. For courage to live as God wants.
(*pause*)
The followers of Jesus have often been
        persecuted
for what they believe
and what they value in life.
May we too be filled with courage
to be worthy followers of the Lamb of God.
Lord, hear us.

3. For those who are leaders in the churches.
(*pause*)
May all who exercise authority and leadership
in the churches
be people of faith and integrity,
committed to the people of God
and renewed in their desire to follow Christ.
Lord, hear us.

4. For those who suffer for their faith.
(*pause*)
Jesus foretold that Peter would die for his faith.
May all who are suffering for what they believe
be comforted by our prayers and active concern;
and may they be consoled and strengthened
by the message of the resurrection.
Lord, hear us.

Priest/Leader

God of all life,
we rejoice that you have called us
to be witnesses of your Son.
Renew our Easter joy
and grant what we need
through Christ our Lord. Amen.

EASTER 4   YEAR C

Priest/Leader

"My sheep hear my voice."
We are the followers of the good shepherd
who gives us eternal life.

We have listened to God's word
and now turn to the Lord for our needs
in the church and in the community.

1. For a deep sense of Easter joy.
(*pause*)
May we continue to be filled with Easter joy
and, like Paul and Barnabas, be so enthused
by the good news of Jesus
that others may come to believe
the message of eternal life.
Lord, hear us.

2. For perseverance in the way of Christ.
(*pause*)
May we remain faithful to the Easter promises,
constant in following the Lord,
who offers living water
to those who are faithful
in serving the Lamb of God.
Lord, hear us.

3. For a desire to listen to the good shepherd.
(*pause*)
Jesus is the good shepherd
whose care is always for his flock.
May we be faithful disciples of the
        good shepherd,
attentive to his teaching
that brings eternal life.
Lord, hear us.

4. For a sense of being the people of God.
(*pause*)
We are the followers of the good shepherd
and no one can steal us from him.
May we deepen our sense of being the
        people of God,
who gave us into the safekeeping of Jesus
that we might learn to live as God wants.
Lord, hear us.

Priest/Leader

God of all ages,
you desire that all people come to salvation.
Help us to be faithful witnesses of your Son.
We ask this through Christ our Lord. Amen.

EASTER 5 YEAR C

Priest/Leader

"By this everyone will know that you are
    my disciples,
if you have love for one another."
God's word has been broken for us
and we are encouraged by its teaching.
We now turn to our God
for what we need.

1. For the gift of encouragement.
(pause)
Paul and Barnabas put fresh hope
into the followers of Jesus,
urging them to persevere in faith.
May we too encourage one another in faith
and in following the way of Christ.
Lord, hear us.

2. For the gift of consolation.
(pause)
The revelation of John strengthened the first
    Christians.
May we too console one another
in times of distress and bereavement,
aware that God has promised to wipe away all tears,
and that all things have been made new in Christ.
Lord, hear us.

3. For the gift of love.
(pause)
Jesus has given us a new commandment—
to love one another.
May we be true to his teaching
that people may recognize us
as disciples of the Lord.
Lord, hear us.

4. For the gift of witness.
(pause)
May we continue to be witnesses to the risen Jesus,
to his teaching and his way;
and by our commitment to gospel values,
may God be glorified
and people everywhere come to faith.
Lord, hear us.

Priest/Leader

God of all consolation,
you have renewed all things in Christ.
Fill us with hope and joy in this Easter time;
and grant what we need
through Christ our Lord. Amen.

EASTER 6 YEAR C

Priest/Leader

"Those who love me will keep my word."
As friends of Jesus,
we have listened to God's word.
Now we turn to our God in prayer,
confident that we will be heard.

1. For an awareness of God's love for all people.
(pause)
God has no favorites,
and no nation or people can claim God as
    their own.
May we learn tolerance of other faiths and cultures,
acknowledging that those who seek justice
    and truth
are pleasing and acceptable to God.
Lord, hear us.

2. For the gift of loving one another.
(pause)
May we take to heart the command to love,
learning from the example of Jesus himself.
May we try to live out this command,
forgiving and accepting one another
as children of God.
Lord, hear us.

3. For a deeper understanding of God's love for us.
(pause)
God's love is measured by the gift of Jesus,
    the only Son
who laid down his life for his friends.
May we grow in understanding
the mystery and meaning of this great love
and respond to it by our own self-giving.
Lord, hear us.

4. For a desire to deepen our friendship with Christ.
(pause)
We are no longer servants but friends of the Lord,
chosen to bear fruit in our world.
May our friendship with our Lord deepen and grow,
reaching to the perfection of loving one another
that God commands.
Lord, hear us.

Priest/Leader

God of love,
you command us to love one another.
Increase our faith
and help us grow in love for one another.
We ask this through Christ our Lord. Amen.

EASTER 7   YEAR C

Priest/Leader

"I made your name known to them."
God's word sustains us and strengthens us in life.
Nourished by its good news,
we turn to our God
for what we need.

1. For a spirit of forgiveness.
(pause)
Stephen forgave those who were stoning him.
May we too have the spirit of forgiveness,
not remembering past faults
but eager to forgive one another
as God forgives us.
Lord, hear us.

2. For a spirit of generosity.
(pause)
The Book of Revelation reminds us of the free gift
the Lord has given us—life forever with God.
May we too be generous toward one another,
certain of the promises of Jesus,
who will bring God's rewards to us all.
Lord, hear us.

3. For a spirit of unity.
(pause)
Jesus tells of his love for his followers,
praying for unity among the disciples.
May we work for the unity Jesus prayed for
so that people everywhere
may know of God's love for all the world.
Lord, hear us.

4. For a spirit of mission.
(pause)
Jesus commands us to witness in his name.
May we not be ashamed of the gospel
but eager to witness to its message,
knowing that we belong to him
as he belongs to God.
Lord, hear us.

Priest/Leader

God of all consolation,
you love us and send us out in the name of your
      Son.
Be with us in our journey through life
and grant what we need
through Christ our Lord. Amen.

THE ASCENSION OF THE LORD

Priest/Leader

"He has put all things under his feet
and has made him the head over all things."
As disciples of Christ
rejoicing in his glorious Ascension,
we come to our God in prayer,
recalling our needs
and those of God's people everywhere.

1. For a greater understanding of God's plan for sal-
    vation.
(*pause*)
May we who are members of Christ's body, the
    church,
grow in understanding the mystery
of God's purposes for the world;
and may we so live as God's people
that we may share the glory that has been promised.
Lord, hear us.

2. For a deep sense of hope.
(*pause*)
The feast of the Ascension
teaches us about hope in God's promises.
May we be confident
in our witnessing to the gospel,
comforted by the presence of Jesus forever.
Lord, hear us.

3. For a desire to be witnesses to the gospel.
(*pause*)
The authority to teach has been given
to the community of disciples.
May we be faithful witnesses to Christ's teaching
so that people everywhere
may hear God's good news for the world.
Lord, hear us.

4. For confidence in Jesus' abiding presence.
(*pause*)
Jesus is the Immanuel—God with us—
who has promised to be among us forever.
May his constant presence in the church
encourage us to live by the commandments of God
and make disciples of all the nations.
Lord, hear us.

Priest/Leader

God of the promises, we worship you
as our ruler and head.
Be our consolation as we await the coming of
    the Lord.
We ask this through Christ our Lord. Amen.

ASCENSION OF THE LORD   YEAR B

Priest/Leader

"He has put all things under his feet
and has made him the head over all things."
As disciples of Christ
rejoicing in his glorious Ascension,
we come to our God in prayer,
recalling our needs
and those of God's people everywhere.

1. For a deep sense of hope.
(*pause*)
The feast of the Ascension
teaches us about hope in God's promises.
May we be confident
in our witnessing to the gospel,
comforted by the presence of Jesus forever.
Lord, hear us.

2. For the gift of unity.
(*pause*)
May we be concerned
about the unity of God's people;
and by our patience and gentleness and
    service,
may we bear with one another
in building up the body of Christ.
Lord, hear us.

3. For a desire to be witnesses to the gospel.
(*pause*)
The authority to teach has been given
to the community of disciples.
May we be faithful witnesses to Christ's
    teaching
so that people everywhere
may hear God's good news for the world.
Lord, hear us.

4. For confidence in proclaiming the good news.
(pause)
Jesus promised signs of hope
to the faithful disciples.
May we who celebrate the Ascension
be confident of Christ's saving power
to confirm our preaching of the gospel.
Lord, hear us.

Priest/Leader

God of the promises, we worship you
as our ruler and head.
Be our consolation as we await the coming of
    the Lord.
We ask this through Christ our Lord. Amen.

ASCENSION OF THE LORD   YEAR C

Priest/Leader

"He has put all things under his feet
and has made him the head over all things."
As disciples of Christ
we come to our God in prayer,
recalling our needs
and those of God's people everywhere.

1. For a deep sense of hope.
(pause)
The feast of the Ascension
teaches us about hope in God's promises.
May we be confident
in our witnessing to the gospel,
comforted by the presence of Jesus forever.
Lord, hear us.

2. For confidence in Christ our High Priest.
(pause)
Jesus is our High Priest
who is in God's presence forever.
May we have confidence in him
who pleads for us before God
until all sin has been destroyed.
Lord, hear us.

3. For a desire to be witnesses to the gospel.
(pause)
The authority to teach has been given
to the community of disciples.
May we be faithful witnesses to Christ's teaching
so that people everywhere
may hear God's good news for the world.
Lord, hear us.

4. For a sense of joy at the Ascension of the Lord.
(pause)
The first Christians were filled with joy.
May we too have a sense of joy,
celebrating God's Holy One
who has gone before us
to be with God forever.
Lord, hear us.

Priest/Leader

God of the promises, we worship you
as our ruler and head.
Be our consolation as we await the coming of the
    Lord.
We ask this through Christ our Lord. Amen.

PENTECOST DAY

PENTECOST SUNDAY   YEAR A

Priest/Leader

Fifty days have passed since Easter.
We welcome God's Spirit among us,
comforting, inspiring, consoling,
and helping us as we pray to God
for what we need.

1. For a desire to make Christ known throughout
      the world.
(*pause*)
The people of Jerusalem heard the good news
in their own languages.
May we be constant in searching for fresh ways
to preach and teach the gospel
to God's people in today's world.
Lord, hear us.

2. For an openness to God's Spirit.
(*pause*)
The Spirit brings new life to the church
and renews the whole world.
May we be open to the gifts of the Spirit,
believing that the church is led by the Spirit
toward a future known only to God.
Lord, hear us.

3. For a spirit of forgiveness.
(*pause*)
The gift of the Spirit is the gift of peace.
May we reach out to our sisters and brothers
with forgiveness and tolerance
and be peacemakers for God in our families,
our communities, and our world.
Lord, hear us.

4. For a sense of joy.
(*pause*)
The Spirit of God sent on Pentecost
filled the disciples with joy.
May we too have that sense of joy
as we witness to God's healing purposes
in the church and in the world.
Lord, hear us.

Priest/Leader

Come, Holy Spirit,
fill us with your loving presence.
Make us strong and constant followers of Jesus,
on fire, like the apostles, with love for his
      good news.
We ask this through Christ our Lord. Amen.

PENTECOST SUNDAY   YEAR B

Priest/Leader

Fifty days have passed since Easter.
We welcome God's Spirit among us,
comforting, inspiring, consoling,
and helping us as we pray to God
for what we need.

1. For a desire to make Christ known throughout
      the world.
(*pause*)
The people of Jerusalem heard the good news
in their own languages.
May we be constant in searching for fresh ways
to preach and teach the gospel
to God's people in today's world.
Lord, hear us.

2. For a desire to live by the Spirit.
(*pause*)
Paul urges us to be led by God's Spirit.
May our lives be so directed by that Spirit
that we may be filled
with love and joy and peace
and all the gifts God sends.
Lord, hear us.

3. For a desire to be witnesses of Jesus.
(*pause*)
Jesus promised to send the Advocate
to strengthen us as faithful witnesses
      of Jesus.
May our celebration of Pentecost
and the gift of the Spirit of truth
encourage us to live by the gospel.
Lord, hear us.

4. For confidence in God's purposes.
(pause)
God's gift of the Spirit
fills us with confidence.
May we be tongues of fire
in the church and in the world,
witnessing in hope to the purposes of God.
Lord, hear us.

Priest/Leader

Come, Holy Spirit,
fill us with your loving presence.
Make us strong and constant followers of Jesus,
on fire, like the apostles, with love for his good news.
We ask this through Christ our Lord. Amen.

PENTECOST SUNDAY   YEAR C

Priest/Leader

Fifty days have passed since Easter.
We welcome God's Spirit among us,
comforting, inspiring, consoling,
and helping us as we pray to God
for what we need.

1. For a desire to make Christ known throughout
      the world.
(pause)
The people of Jerusalem heard the good news
in their own languages.
May we be constant in searching for fresh ways
to preach and teach the gospel
to God's people in today's world.
Lord, hear us.

2. For a desire to live by the Spirit.
(pause)
Paul teaches us that we are God's children,
living by the Spirit of God.
May we deepen our desire to witness to
      the gospel,
rejoicing that Abba God is our Father,
who invites us to share the glory of Christ.
Lord, hear us.

3. For an openness to God's Spirit.
(pause)
The Spirit brings new life to the church
and renews the whole world.
May we be open to the prompting of the Spirit
to keep the commandments of Jesus,
comforted by the presence of the Spirit with
      us forever.
Lord, hear us.

4. For a sense of renewal.
(pause)
God's gift of the Spirit is a gift of love,
consoling us with God's promise
to make a home with us.
May we resolve to be tongues of fire
witnessing to God's truth in our world.
Lord, hear us.

Priest/Leader

Come, Holy Spirit,
fill us with your loving presence.
Make us strong and constant followers of Jesus,
on fire, like the apostles, with love for his good news.
We ask this through Christ our Lord. Amen.

FEAST OF THE HOLY TRINITY

Priest/Leader

"God sent the Son into the world
that the world might be saved."
As sisters and brothers of Jesus,
we approach our God with confidence,
asking for those things we need
as God's children in God's world.

1. For a sense of God's kindness.
(pause)
God is revealed in the scriptures
as a God of tenderness and compassion.
May we have a sense of God's kindness,
rejoicing in God's readiness to forgive us
by our desire to live by the commandments.
Lord, hear us.

2. For a desire to love one another.
(pause)
Paul urges us to help one another.
May we be conscious
of God's love for us in Christ;
and may we strive for unity and peace,
living in the fellowship that is God's gift to us.
Lord, hear us.

3. For an awareness of God's love.
(pause)
The gift of God's Son
is the measure of God's love for the world.
May we grow in our awareness of God's love
and resolve to bear witness to the truth of God
in our world.
Lord, hear us.

4. For the gift of deep faith.
(pause)
Jesus came not to condemn the world but
    to save it.
On this feast of the Trinity
may our faith in God deepen
so that all people may come to believe
in the name of God's only Son.
Lord, hear us.

Priest/Leader

Creator God, may your name be held holy.
May your kingdom come!
Listen to the prayers we make this day
through Christ our Lord. Amen.

TRINITY SUNDAY   YEAR B

Priest/Leader

"You did not receive a spirit of slavery,…
but you have received a spirit of adoption."
With renewed confidence
we approach our God for what we need
as God's people in God's world.

1. For a respect for the name of God.
(pause)
We worship God—three yet one—
who is Lord of all the universe.
May our respect for God
and our desire to live by the commandments
mark us as God's faithful people in the world.
Lord, hear us.

2. For a sense of belonging to God's family.
(pause)
Paul teaches us that we are moved by the Spirit
to call God "Abba, Father."
May we rejoice that we are no longer slaves
but members of God's family,
coheirs, with Christ, of God's glory.
Lord, hear us.

3. For a desire to spread the good news.
(pause)
Jesus commands us to make disciples
of all the nations.
May we be faithful witnesses
of the way of Jesus
in what we teach and how we live.
Lord, hear us.

4. For an awareness of Christ's presence with us.
(pause)
May we rejoice in the constant presence
of Jesus with his people.
May we confess his authority in heaven and on earth

observing the commandments
given to us by the Son of God.
Lord, hear us.

Priest/Leader

Creator God, may your name be held holy!
May your kingdom come!
Listen to the prayers we make this day
through Christ our Lord. Amen.

TRINITY SUNDAY   YEAR C

Priest/Leader

"God's love has been poured into our hearts."
The word of God nourishes us
and strengthens us in our pilgrimage through life.
Nourished by that word,
we turn to the Lord for what we need.

1. For the gift of wisdom.
(pause)
God's gift of wisdom has been with creation
from the beginning of time.
May we be filled with that wisdom
that we may discern what is just in life
according to God's will.
Lord, hear us.

2. For the gift of peace.
(pause)
God has declared us at peace

because of our faith in Christ.
By our perseverance in suffering
may we experience the hope and love
that is promised by God.
Lord, hear us.

3. For a desire to know the truth.
(pause)
The Holy Spirit leads us to the truth.
May we never be ashamed of the truth
    we profess
but seek to glorify God
by living as God's children
who witness the teaching of the gospel.
Lord, hear us.

4. For an awareness of our need for
    God's Spirit.
(pause)
Jesus promises us the Spirit,
who will bring to completion
the teaching of the Lord.
May we welcome God's Spirit into our lives
to help us live by the gospel of the Lord.
Lord, hear us.

Priest/Leader

Creator God, may your name be held holy!
May your kingdom come!
Listen to the prayers we make this day
through Christ our Lord. Amen.

FEAST OF THE
BODY AND BLOOD OF CHRIST

BODY AND BLOOD OF CHRIST
YEAR A

Priest/Leader

"Whoever eats of this bread will live forever."
The promises of Jesus
comfort us on this day of celebration.
With renewed confidence,
we approach our God for what we need.

1. For an awareness of God's gifts.
(pause)
God cared for the people of Israel,
providing them with nourishment
during their wanderings in the desert.
May we too be aware of God's care for us
and the gifts God gives us in life.
Lord, hear us.

2. For unity among Christians.
(pause)
The bread we share
is a communion with the body of Christ.
May we work for harmony among his disciples,
seeking the unity that is offered
in the sacrament of Christ's body and blood.
Lord, hear us.

3. For an understanding of Jesus, the bread
    of life.
(pause)
Jesus has promised life forever
to those who eat his flesh and drink his blood.
May our sharing in this Eucharist
be a sign of our deeper commitment
to follow his teaching.
Lord, hear us.

4. For a desire to live for Christ.
(pause)
Life is God's gift to us; life is Christ's promise
    to us.
May our belonging to this community
and our celebration of this Eucharist
be a sign of our desire
to live with Christ forever.
Lord, hear us.

Priest/Leader

God of the covenant,
you give us this sacrament as a sign of your love
    for us.
May we grow in love, eager to worship you
by our care for one another.
We ask this through Christ our Lord. Amen.

BODY AND BLOOD OF CHRIST
YEAR B

Priest/Leader

Jesus is our High Priest
whose precious blood established
an everlasting covenant with God.
As people of the covenant,
we bring our prayers before the Lord.

1. For a desire to live as God commands.
(pause)
With the blood of animals
the people of Israel sealed the ancient covenant
    with God.
May we who are sealed in the new covenant,
by the blood of Christ,
renew our desire to live as God commands.
Lord, hear us.

2. For a greater understanding of the sacrifice of
    Christ.
(pause)
The blood of Christ makes us holy before God
for lives of service to God and to one another.
May we grow in our understanding
of what Christ has achieved for us
by his life and death.
Lord, hear us.

3. For a deeper respect and love of the Eucharist.
(pause)
Jesus commanded us to share his body and blood
in memory of him.
May we grow in our reverence for the Eucharist
and live out its command of love
in all that we do.
Lord, hear us.

4. For a desire to be faithful to the covenant.
(pause)
We are nourished by the body and blood of the Lord.
May our sharing in this sacrament
renew our desire to live more faithfully
as followers of the Christ
who shed his blood for the life of all.
Lord, hear us.

Priest/Leader

God of the covenant,
you give us this sacrament as a sign of your love
    for us.
May we grow in love, eager to serve you.
We ask this through Christ our Lord. Amen.

BODY AND BLOOD OF CHRIST
YEAR C

Priest/Leader

"Do this in remembrance of me."
As God's people, we gather to share the good news
of Jesus' life and death.
Strengthened by God's word,
we turn to our God in prayer.

1. For thanksgiving for all God's gifts.
(pause)
Melchizedech, priest of God,
offered bread and wine,
symbols of all we need in life.
May our celebration of the Eucharist
reflect our thanksgiving for all God's gifts.
Lord, hear us.

2. For a renewed sense of belonging in
    the church.
(pause)
Paul teaches us what he received from
    the Lord.
May our sharing in the Eucharist
deepen our sense of belonging in the church,
sharing the body and blood of the Lord
and proclaiming his death until he comes again.
Lord, hear us.

3. For confidence in God's gifts.
(pause)
Twelve baskets were collected,
signs of God's generous love.
May our celebration of the Eucharist
recall for us God's faithfulness
and renew our confidence in God's care.
Lord, hear us.

4. For a desire to live out what we celebrate.
(pause)
Jesus fed the five thousand
from the few resources he had.
May we be strengthened in the Eucharist
to live out his command
to care for one another.
Lord, hear us.

Priest/Leader

God of all ages,
you renew your people
through the mystery of the Eucharist.
Help us be faithful to its teaching
through Christ our Lord. Amen.

FEAST OF THE SACRED HEART OF JESUS

SACRED HEART OF JESUS YEAR A

Priest/Leader

"My yoke is easy, and my burden light."
The Sacred Heart of Jesus
is a sign of God's unending love.
With confidence in our God,
we bring our needs before the Lord.

1. For a desire to keep God's commandments.
(pause)
God is the faithful one
who rescued the people from slavery
    in Egypt.
As a nation consecrated to God
may we be known as God's faithful people
who keep the commandments of the Lord.
Lord, hear us.

2. For a desire to live in love.
(pause)
God's love for us is revealed
in the gift of Jesus, God's Son,
the sacrifice that takes away our sin.
May we deepen our desire to live in love
that God may live in us.
Lord, hear us.

3. For an openness to God's ways.
(pause)
The Father is blessed
for revealing how we are to live.
May we be open to God's ways,
faithful to the example of Jesus
and to all that the gospel teaches.
Lord, hear us.

4. For trust in God's kindness.
(pause)
Jesus calls us to be gentle and humble,
accepting his teaching that brings us peace.
May we trust always
in the kindness of our God
whose yoke is easy and whose burden
    is light.
Lord, hear us.

Priest/Leader

God of all consolation,
we bless you for your love and kindness.
Grant what we need
to be faithful servants of your Son.
For he is Lord, forever and ever. Amen.

SACRED HEART OF JESUS YEAR B

Priest/Leader

"They will look on the one whom they have
    pierced."
The love of God is everlasting;
the word of God remains forever.
Comforted by that word,
we bring our needs before our God.

1. For an awareness of God's love for us.
(pause)
Hosea reminds us
of God's deep love for each of us.
May we grow in understanding God's kindness
and learn to love one another
as God first loved us.
Lord, hear us.

2. For a deeper faith in God.
(pause)
May we grow in respect
for the majesty and the power of our God;
and may our faith in God's goodness
help us grow strong in faith
until we are filled with the fullness of God.
Lord, hear us.

3. For a spirit of self-giving.
(pause)
Jesus is the Lamb of God
sacrificed for us on the cross.
May we learn from the love of Jesus
to be servants of one another
in the church and in the community.
Lord, hear us.

4. For a desire to witness to the truth.
(pause)
May we be people of the truth,

witnesses to the life and teaching of Jesus.
May the blood and water from his side
be for us signs of his great love
to comfort and strengthen us in
      life's journey.
Lord, hear us.

Priest/Leader

God of the promises,
on this feast of the Sacred Heart,
help us to respond to your love;
and grant what we need.
Through Christ our Lord. Amen.

SACRED HEART OF JESUS   YEAR C

Priest/Leader

"I myself will be the shepherd of
      my sheep."
The feast of the Sacred Heart of Jesus
celebrates God's love for us in Christ.
Comforted by its teaching,
we turn to our God for what we need.

1. For a sense of God's consolation.
(*pause*)
God is the shepherd
who gathers the sheep and protects them.
May we have a sense of God's care
and be comforted
by the promises of our God.
Lord, hear us.

2. For an appreciation of God's love for us.
(*pause*)
God's love has been poured into our hearts
by the Spirit given to us.
May we grow in understanding God's love
that rescued us from death,
reconciling us to God and to one another.
Lord, hear us.

3. For the gift of forgiveness and acceptance.
(*pause*)
The gospel teaches us the lengths
to which God goes to show love and forgiveness.
May we be moved by God's love
to accept and forgive one another
as God accepts us.
Lord, hear us.

4. For a spirit of repentance.
(*pause*)
Jesus spoke of heaven rejoicing
when people turn from their sins.
May we acknowledge sin in our lives
and resolve to overcome its power
in ourselves and in our world.
Lord, hear us.

Priest/Leader

God of love,
you call us to live by the teaching of the gospel.
Fill us with love this day
and grant what we need
through Christ our Lord. Amen.

SUNDAYS IN ORDINARY TIME

Priest/Leader

"Here is the Lamb of God
who takes away the sin of the world."
The word of God gives us life and joy.
We have listened to its teaching
and professed our faith.
With confidence, we turn to our God
for what we need.

1. For a desire to be God's witnesses.
(pause)
We are God's people, called to be a light to the
      nations.
By our faithfulness to the teaching of the
      scriptures,
may God be glorified
and all people acknowledge God's chosen one
as Lord of life.
Lord, hear us.

2. For a desire to be of service.
(pause)
God calls us to be servants of one another
in the community of saints
that is the church all over the world.
May our love and acceptance of one another
make us worthy to be called the people of God.
Lord, hear us.

3. For a desire to be true followers of Jesus.
(pause)
Jesus is the Lamb of God
who takes away the sin of the world.
May we be faithful followers of the Lamb
refusing to be controlled by sin and evil
and eager, like him, to be a light for the world.
Lord, hear us.

4. For a desire to make Christ known in the world.
(pause)
Jesus is the chosen one of God,
the model of faithful service.
May we so follow his teaching and example
that people everywhere will come to know
the truth about God and about the Christ.
Lord, hear us.

Priest/Leader

God of the promises,
help us to be faithful followers of your Son,
who lives and reigns
forever and ever. Amen.

Priest/Leader

"I will make you fish for all people."
God's word challenges us to take seriously
the way of Jesus.
Nourished by its teaching
we look to our God
for what we need.

1. For a sense of joy in following the Lord.
(pause)
We are the people of God,
called to walk in the light.
May we be filled with joy,
bringing the good news to others
that all may share the freedom promised by God.
Lord, hear us.

2. For unity in the church.
(pause)
Paul appeals for unity
among those who preach the gospel
in Christ's body, the church.
May we strive to accept one another
as God accepts us, in Christ crucified.
Lord, hear us.

3. For a sense of repentance.
(pause)
Jesus calls us to repent
and believe the good news.
May we have courage to follow his teaching,
bringing light to the world
and healing to its people.
Lord, hear us.

4. For an eagerness to follow the Lord's call.
(pause)
Like Peter, Andrew, James, and John,
we too are invited to follow the Lord

and be part of God's plan to save all people.
May we be constant in our witness to the gospel
by the integrity of our lives.
Lord, hear us.

Priest/Leader

God of the promises,
you bring us joy in following your way.
Listen to the prayers we make
through Christ our Lord. Amen.

SUNDAY 4   YEAR A

Priest/Leader

"Rejoice and be glad
for your reward is great in heaven."
God's powerful word nourishes our spirit
and sustains us in our journey through life.
Strengthened by its teaching
we turn to our God for our needs.

1. For a desire to live by the truth.
(pause)
God commands us to live lives of integrity and
    humility,
understanding that God's ways are not our ways.
May we live by the truth of the scripture,
finding peace and fulfillment
in obedience to the commandments of God.
Lord, hear us.

2. For a desire to understand God's purposes.
(pause)
God's ways are unknown to us
and God's purposes are hidden from us.
May we grow in trust of our God
who has declared unimportant
what people regard as important in
    our world.
Lord, hear us.

3. For a desire to live as God wants.
(pause)
In the Sermon on the Mount,
Jesus teaches us what is of value in life.
May our response be one of generous service
and a desire to understand

how we are to live as children of our God.
Lord, hear us.

4. For a desire to live by the Beatitudes of Jesus.
(pause)
May the teaching of Jesus
so fill our hearts
that the gospel values he preached and lived
may become part of the fabric of our lives
in what we do and what we consider important.
Lord, hear us.

Priest/Leader

God of all consolation,
your Son is the way to life.
Help us to follow his teaching
in how we live and what we value.
We ask this through Christ our Lord. Amen.

SUNDAY 5   YEAR A

Priest/Leader

"You are the light of the world."
God's word has been broken for us
and we are nourished by its teaching.
Now we turn to our God
for what we need in the church
and in the community.

1. For a spirit of generosity.
(pause)
God commands us to share what we have
and to be generous toward those in need.
May we be a people of God worthy of
    the name,
responding to God's call
by our charity, our giving, and our love.
Lord, hear us.

2. For a renewed faith in Christ crucified.
(pause)
Paul preached Christ crucified
and we too acknowledge the Christ
as central to our lives.
May the message of the cross encourage us
to be faithful in following his way.
Lord, hear us.

3. For a desire to be the salt of the earth.
(*pause*)
May we be strengthened in our desire
to be the people of the gospel;
and may our faithfulness to its teaching
make our world and our communities
places of justice and truth.
Lord, hear us.

4. For a desire to be the light of the world.
(*pause*)
May our lives as Christians
so reflect the teaching of Jesus
that all people will be attracted to the gospel
and come to know the truth about God
and about the Christ.
Lord, hear us.

Priest/Leader

God of all truth,
you command us to be salt and light in our world.
Help us to be faithful in following your Son.
We ask this through Christ our Lord. Amen.

SUNDAY 6   YEAR A

Priest/Leader

"I have come not to abolish
but to fulfill."
God's word is food for our journey in life.
Strengthened by its message
we turn to our God for what we need.

1. For the gift of keeping the commandments.
(*pause*)
The commandments of God
bring life and fulfillment.
May we be strong in our observance of God's law;
and may the Lord guide us
in the choices we make in life.
Lord, hear us.

2. For an awareness of God's purposes.
(*pause*)
The hidden purposes of God
work for our happiness and our wholeness.
May God's Spirit be at work in us

to teach us what is needed in our lives
to reach what God has promised.
Lord, hear us.

3. For a desire to live by the gospel.
(*pause*)
The demands of the gospel are strong,
affecting what we value in life.
May we be conscious of how we are to live,
reaching out to one another with forgiveness,
according to the commandments of God.
Lord, hear us.

4. For the gift of speaking the truth.
(*pause*)
May we be a people
committed to the truth;
and may each of us strive
for that honesty, truthfulness, and just living
that Jesus commanded of those who would
     follow him.
Lord, hear us.

Priest/Leader

God of all truth,
in you nothing is hidden.
Help us to be faithful followers of your Son.
For he is Lord, forever and ever. Amen.

SUNDAY 7   YEAR A

Priest/Leader

"Be perfect, therefore,
as your heavenly Father is perfect."
God's word calls us to lives of perfection.
Conscious of our littleness before God,
we turn to our Lord for what we need.

1. For a desire to keep God's commandments.
(*pause*)
God requires us to be holy
by keeping the commandments.
May we strive to love one another,
not bearing grudges but forgiving one
     another
as God commands.
Lord, hear us.

2. For a desire to belong to Christ.
(pause)
We are called to be temples of God,
worthy of the Spirit who dwells within us.
May we be diligent in doing what God wants,
proclaiming that we belong to Christ
even when this is foolish by human reckoning.
Lord, hear us.

3. For a true spirit of forgiveness.
(pause)
May we learn from the teaching of Jesus
to be generous in our forgiveness,
to acknowledge faults in ourselves and others
and to live in peace with one another
for the sake of the gospel.
Lord, hear us.

4. For a desire to love our enemies.
(pause)
The command of Jesus is that we love even
    our enemies.
By God's grace, may we be moved
to forgive people who have wronged us;
and, especially in families,
may the love of Jesus bring healing and forgiveness.
Lord, hear us.

Priest/Leader

God of love,
you require us to be perfect
for your sake.
Help us to be faithful followers of your Holy One.
For he is Lord, forever and ever. Amen.

SUNDAY 8   YEAR A

Priest/Leader

"Do not worry about tomorrow,
for tomorrow will bring worries of its own."
The gospel encourages our trust in God's kindness.
Strengthened by its teaching, we approach our God
with our prayers and needs.

1. For renewed faith in God's love for each of us.
(pause)
God will not abandon us nor forget us.

May the teaching of God's word
console us in time of trouble;
and may we grow in faith and love,
confident of God's care for each of us.
Lord, hear us.

2. For a desire to be good servants of the Lord.
(pause)
We are servants of Jesus,
entrusted by him to live lives worthy of God's love.
May we be good servants of the Lord,
witnessing to the gospel by how we live
and what we value.
Lord, hear us.

3. For a right attitude toward possessions.
(pause)
May we take to heart the teaching of the gospel,
avoiding excess in how we live;
and by attitudes toward what we eat and what
    we wear,
may we deepen our faith in our God
who cares for all the creatures of the world.
Lord, hear us.

4. For a desire to serve God only.
(pause)
We cannot be slaves of two masters.
May the teaching of Jesus so move us
that we will determine to serve God rather than
    money,
setting our hearts on what is required
for the coming of God's reign.
Lord, hear us.

Priest/Leader

God of all consolation,
may your kingdom come!
Listen to the prayers we make; and grant them.
We ask this through Christ our Lord. Amen.

SUNDAY 9   YEAR A

Priest/Leader

"Be like a wise man who built his house on rock."
God's word has been broken for us
and its teaching nourishes us for life's journey.

Strengthened by its message,
we turn to our God for what we need.

1. For a desire to live as God wants.
(*pause*)
May we be filled with a desire to do God's will
and to live according to the scriptures
so that, holding fast to the teaching of the Lord,
we may be worthy of the blessings
promised by our God.
Lord, hear us.

2. For a deeper faith in God.
(*pause*)
Faith makes us right with God.
May our faith in Christ grow each day
and may we witness to what we believe
by lives that reflect the teaching of the gospel
and the commandments of the Lord.
Lord, hear us.

3. For a determination to work for God's reign.
(*pause*)
God's reign is promised to those who do
        God's will.
May our lives in the church and in the
        community
be founded on a desire to live God's way:
striving for justice in society
and caring for those in need.
Lord, hear us.

4. For an eagerness to listen to God's word.
(*pause*)
May we be open to God's word and God's teaching
in the scriptures and in the community;
and, like a house built on rock,
may we be strong in our journey of faith
through all of life.
Lord, hear us.

Priest/Leader

God of all creation,
we thank you for your gift of faith.
Strengthen us in our journey
and grant what we need.
We ask this through Christ our Lord. Amen.

Priest/Leader

"Follow me," says the Lord.
God's powerful word is food for our journey
        in faith.
Nourished by its teaching, we turn to
        our God
for what we need.

1. For a desire to know God's will.
(*pause*)
May we be constant in seeking God's will
for the church and for the community.
And may our love and service
be deep and lasting
until the Lord comes.
Lord, hear us.

2. For the gifts of faith and hope.
(*pause*)
Like Abraham, our father in faith,
may we be filled with the gift of hope,
believing the promises of God,
who raised Jesus to life,
reconciling us to our God and to our world.
Lord, hear us.

3. For a desire to follow Jesus.
(*pause*)
Like Matthew, may we follow Jesus,
alert to his call and eager to be his disciples;
and, like Matthew, may we be open
to changes in lifestyle
in how we live and what we consider
        important.
Lord, hear us.

4. For a right attitude toward our religion.
(*pause*)
May we not be satisfied by ritual alone,
but may we seek to reflect our relationship
        with our God,
seeking God's justice more than empty worship
through our care for others,
especially those in most need.
Lord, hear us.

Priest/Leader

God of our ancestors, you demand mercy, not ritual.
Strengthen our resolve to live by your way
and grant what we need.
We ask this through Christ our Lord. Amen.

SUNDAY 11   YEAR A

Priest/Leader

"I bore you on eagles' wings."
Our God is a God who cares for us and loves us.
Strengthened by God's word,
we bring our needs before the Lord.

1. For a sense of belonging to God.
(pause)
God has declared us a holy people,
a nation consecrated to the Lord.
May our sense of belonging to God
be reflected in lives of faithfulness
to what God wants.
Lord, hear us.

2. For joyful trust in our God.
(pause)
Jesus has died for us
and reconciled us to our God.
May we be filled with joyful trust
in God's goodness
and live always as people of hope.
Lord, hear us.

3. For a sense of mission in the world.
(pause)
We are commanded to bring healing to our world.
May we be a people of joy and hope,
bringing peace, forgiveness,
and a sense of purpose
to our restless world.
Lord, hear us.

4. For renewed faith in God's purposes.
(pause)
May we be true followers of Jesus,
proclaiming God's reign in our world.
And may people everywhere learn
of God's purposes

by our faithfulness to gospel teaching.
Lord, hear us.

Priest/Leader

God of the promises,
grant what we need
to live as disciples of Jesus,
who is Lord, forever and ever. Amen.

SUNDAY 12   YEAR A

Priest/Leader

"Do not be afraid."
The good news of God's word encourages us
to approach our God with love and confidence.
We now reflect on what we need
as God's people in God's world.

1. For confidence in God's love.
(pause)
Jeremiah, the prophet of God,
committed his cause to the Lord,
confident of God's goodness and care.
May we too learn to trust our God
and turn to the Lord in times of trouble.
Lord, hear us.

2. For an awareness of what God has done for us.
(pause)
Through Adam's fault,
the power of sin entered the world.
May we be conscious
of what God has done for us in Christ,
breaking the bonds of sin in our lives.
Lord, hear us.

3. For the strength to overcome fear.
(pause)
When we are afraid for our world,
our families, and ourselves,
may we be consoled by the teaching
that God is ruler of all the world
and Lord of all that is and is to come.
Lord, hear us.

4. For courage to proclaim the truth.
(pause)

We are commanded to proclaim the truth
about God and about the Christ.
By the integrity of our lives,
may we be authentic witnesses
to the teaching of Jesus.
Lord, hear us.

Priest/Leader

God of all consolation,
you free us from fear and give us confidence in life.
Grant what we need
through Christ our Lord. Amen.

SUNDAY 13   YEAR A

Priest/Leader

"Consider yourselves alive to God in Christ Jesus."
The good news of God's word
fills us with hope
as we recall what God has done for us.
In a spirit of confidence, we turn to the Lord
for what we need.

1. For the gift of hospitality.
(pause)
May we be hospitable in our lives,
caring for those who are in need;
and may we be generous
toward those in our society
without love and without hope.
Lord, hear us.

2. For a desire to live a new life in Christ.
(pause)
In baptism, we were raised to new life in Christ.
May we be constant in overcoming
the power of sin in our lives;
and by our faithfulness to the gospel
may we proclaim that we live for Christ.
Lord, hear us.

3. For a desire to share what we have.
(pause)
May we be moved
by the teaching of the gospel
to consider our attitude to what we own;
and may we learn to share our abundance

with those who have less in our world.
Lord, hear us.

4. For the grace to make right decisions in life.
(pause)
Jesus taught us that the cost of discipleship
is to carry a cross.
May his teaching guide us constantly
so that what we basically value in life
may accord with what God wants.
Lord, hear us.

Priest/Leader

Generous God,
your Son died to show his love for us.
May we too be generous in your service
and in caring for others.
We ask this through Christ our Lord. Amen.

SUNDAY 14   YEAR A

Priest/Leader

"My yoke is easy, and my burden is light."
God's word challenges yet comforts us.
Nourished by its teaching,
we turn to the Lord
for what we need
in the church and in the world.

1. For peace in our world.
(pause)
We rejoice because our God brings peace.
May our faith in God's goodness
grow stronger each day;
and may we work for peace in our world
as God commands.
Lord, hear us.

2. For a desire to live by God's Spirit.
(pause)
May we be faithful to our baptism promises
and so desire to live God's way
that the Holy Spirit who has made a home
    in us
may possess our lives
and guide us in what we do.
Lord, hear us.

3. For a spirit of humility before God.
(*pause*)
May we be humble toward the Lord,
aware of God's power in heaven and on earth;
and may we be conscious of our littleness
in God's presence
and the immensity of God's mysterious love.
Lord, hear us.

4. For an awareness of God's kindness.
(*pause*)
May we be strong in faith
and in living the gospel,
acknowledging that the kindness of our God
makes the yoke easy
and the burden light.
Lord, hear us.

Priest/Leader

God of all kindness,
you bless your people in life and in death.
Make us eager to live your way
and to proclaim your truth
in all that we do.
We ask this through Christ our Lord. Amen.

SUNDAY 15   YEAR A

Priest/Leader

"Let anyone with ears listen!"
God's word has been broken for us
and we have listened to its teaching.
Now we reflect on its meaning for us,
turning to the Lord for what we need.

1. For a deeper understanding of God's word.
(*pause*)
May we grow in understanding
the word of God revealed to us.
May we learn to obey its teaching
in the church and in the world
so that God's will may be done.
Lord, hear us.

2. For a deeper appreciation of God's creation.
(*pause*)
All creation witnesses to God's purposes.

May we always respect our universe
and from its beauty, integrity, and nature
deepen our understanding
of how God wants us to treat our world.
Lord, hear us.

3. For a desire to live the way of Jesus.
(*pause*)
May we be guided by the teaching of Jesus
in all that we value
and hold dearest;
and by our living the gospel,
may others be drawn to the truth of God.
Lord, hear us.

4. For the coming of God's reign.
(*pause*)
The teaching of Jesus reveals to us
God's purposes for ourselves and for our world.
May we be faithful followers of Jesus,
listening to his teaching and bearing fruit
by our obedience to God's word.
Lord, hear us.

Priest/Leader

God of the promises,
may your kingdom come!
Help us to be faithful to your word,
producing a rich harvest
in the church and in the world.
We ask this through Christ our Lord. Amen.

SUNDAY 16   YEAR A

Priest/Leader

"The Spirit helps us in our weakness."
Nourished by God's word
and comforted by God's Spirit,
we turn in prayer to our God
for what we need in the church
and in the world.

1. For a sense of God's majesty.
(*pause*)
May we be humble in the Lord's presence,
aware of God's power and might,
yet mindful of God's gentleness

and the command to act justly
toward one another.
Lord, hear us.

2. For an openness to God's Spirit.
(*pause*)
May we welcome the Spirit of God
into our lives;
and may we be open to that Spirit
when we are confused or anxious
about what to say or how to pray.
Lord, hear us.

3. For a sense of the mystery of God's purposes.
(*pause*)
God's purposes are hidden
like seed in the ground.
May we be confident of God's love,
living by the teaching of Jesus
so that God's will for us may be done.
Lord, hear us.

4. For a desire for the coming of
        God's reign.
(*pause*)
May we be eager for the coming
of God's reign;
and by lives that reflect gospel values
may God be glorified
in our community and in our world.
Lord, hear us.

Priest/Leader

God of the universe,
may your kingdom come!
Help us to do your will and to be faithful to your
        teaching.
We ask this through Christ our Lord.
        Amen.

SUNDAY 17   YEAR A

Priest/Leader

"I give you a wise and discerning mind,"
        says the Lord.
God's word has been broken for us
and God's wisdom has filled our minds.

With confidence, we turn to the Lord
for what we need.

1. For the gift of wisdom.
(*pause*)
Like Solomon, the leader in Israel,
may we be people of discernment,
learning to judge what is right in God's sight;
and by lives open to the Spirit
may we always be pleasing to our God.
Lord, hear us.

2. For a desire to imitate Christ.
(*pause*)
Jesus is our brother,
the head of the community called the church.
May we imitate him as our eldest brother
and by our generosity and love
come to the glory promised by God.
Lord, hear us.

3. For enthusiasm in following the
        way of Jesus.
(*pause*)
May we be moved by the teaching of Jesus
to be enthusiastic and generous
in seeking God's reign,
eager for its coming in our church
and in our world.
Lord, hear us.

4. For tolerance in the church.
(*pause*)
Jesus is Lord and head of the church
who values in his household things old
        and new.
May we learn to be tolerant of one another
as we strive to discover God's will
for how we are to live.
Lord, hear us.

Priest/Leader

God of the universe,
teach us your ways.
Fill us with your wisdom
and help us to love one another.
We ask this through Christ our Lord.
        Amen.

SUNDAY 18   YEAR A

Priest/Leader

"Who will separate us
from the love of Christ?"
This is the good news
that we have heard.
God's word has nourished us
and we turn to our God for what we need.

1. For confidence in God's goodness.
(pause)
May we never lose sight
of God's generous goodness and love.
And may we be comforted
by God's promises
to the church and to all people.
Lord, hear us.

2. For a renewed sense of unity with Christ.
(pause)
Paul teaches us that nothing can separate
    us from Christ.
May this teaching renew our sense of unity
with Christ and with one another;
and may it sustain us in times of suffering,
distress, and loss.
Lord, hear us.

3. For an awareness of the need for prayer.
(pause)
Jesus went to a lonely place
seeking consolation and strength.
May we grow in our life of prayer,
trusting our God to comfort us
in times of need.
Lord, hear us.

4. For generosity toward others.
(pause)
Jesus fed the five thousand
from the few resources he had.
May we learn to imitate the Master,
knowing that the little we have
can become abundant in God's sight.
Lord, hear us.

Priest/Leader

God of all goodness,
you are bountiful to your people.
Help us to be your faithful followers
in the church and in the community.
We ask this through Christ our Lord. Amen.

SUNDAY 19   YEAR A

Priest/Leader

"Truly you are the Son of God."
God's word has been broken for us
and we are comforted by its teaching.
We recall the needs of our church
and our world
and present them to the Lord.

1. For an appreciation of God's gentleness
    and love.
(pause)
God is revealed to Isaiah
in the sound of a gentle breeze.
May we grow in reverence and love
toward our God who is revealed
in gentleness and tenderness.
Lord, hear us.

2. For the Jewish people.
(pause)
Paul prayed for the Jewish people
and we too commend them
to our loving God.
May they be faithful to the ancient covenant
and remain steadfast in their longing for
    God's reign.
Lord, hear us.

3. For a deepening of our life of prayer.
(pause)
Jesus went off into the hills to pray.
May we too relish time spent in prayer;
and may these times of reflection and peace
give us renewed strength
on our journey with God.
Lord, hear us.

4. For the courage to follow Jesus.
(pause)
Like Peter, may we have the courage
to follow Jesus
even when we are afraid;
and may our faith in Christ sustain us
especially in times of stress and fear.
Lord, hear us.

Priest/Leader

God of storm and earthquake,
you are mighty and powerful,
yet you reveal yourself to the little ones of the earth.
Hear the prayers we make to you
through Christ our Lord. Amen.

SUNDAY 20   YEAR A

Priest/Leader

"Have mercy on me, Lord, Son of David."
Nourished by God's word,
we approach the Lord in a spirit of humility,
seeking what we need
for our church and our world.

1. For an openness to people of other faiths.
(pause)
We believe in our God who is Ruler of all the earth,
who cares for all the people of the world.
May we respect people of other faiths
who search for truth and meaning
in their journey through life.
Lord, hear us.

2. For the Jewish people.
(pause)
The Jewish people are God's covenanted people.
May we be conscious of their special place
in God's plan of salvation;
and may we be vigilant in promoting harmony
among people of different traditions and cultures.
Lord, hear us.

3. For perseverance in prayer.
(pause)
Like the woman in the gospel story,
may we be confident in prayer

and grow in faith;
and may we be open to what God wants in our lives
as the beginning of all our prayer.
Lord, hear us.

4. For the grace to be faithful witnesses.
(pause)
May the community that is called the church
be a faithful witness to its Lord;
and, following the example of Jesus,
may we be open to all people of good will
who show us the purposes of our God.
Lord, hear us.

Priest/Leader

God of the promises,
you surprise us with the answers to our prayers.
Help us to be good servants of your Son.
We ask this through Christ our Lord. Amen.

SUNDAY 21   YEAR A

Priest/Leader

"You are the Messiah, the Son of the living God."
God's word nourishes us in our faith journey.
We now recall the needs of our church
and our communities
as we turn to the Lord in prayer.

1. For leaders in the churches.
(pause)
May those who exercise leadership in the churches
be people of faith and wisdom,
alert to the gifts God gives to all;
and by their preaching the truth about God
may they strengthen God's people everywhere.
Lord, hear us.

2. For an awareness of God's majesty and
     goodness.
(pause)
With Paul, may we be filled with wonder
at the majesty of God.
May we always reverence the living God
whose nature and purposes are beyond
our words and imagination.
Lord, hear us.

3. For preachers and teachers in the churches.
(*pause*)
We pray for those who preach and teach
in our churches, schools, and places of learning.
May they be constant in pointing to the Christ
    of God;
and may we encourage them and support them
in their ministry and work.
Lord, hear us.

4. For a deeper faith among all who believe.
(*pause*)
May all of us be renewed in faith this day
and, like Peter, who confessed Jesus as
    God's Son,
renew our commitment to follow the way
    of Christ
by lives that take seriously
the teaching of the gospel.
Lord, hear us.

Priest/Leader

Living God and Father,
you have revealed yourself to us
in Jesus your Son.
Help us to follow his way and his teaching,
for he is Lord, forever and ever. Amen.

SUNDAY 22   YEAR A

Priest/Leader

"Let them…take up their cross and follow me."
God's word nourishes us,
giving us the strength and the courage
to live as God wants.
Refreshed by its teaching, we approach our God
for what we need.

1. For the gift to persevere in God's service.
(*pause*)
Jeremiah, the prophet of God,
teaches that God's call is a call to service.
May we be faithful in following God's way,
supporting one another
by the values we own and the truths we profess.
Lord, hear us.

2. For a desire to discover God's will.
(*pause*)
May we always seek to find God's will
in the church and in the community;
and may we have the courage to be guided by
    God's call,
seeking the perfection God wants
in how we live.
Lord, hear us.

3. For an acceptance of the cross of Christ.
(*pause*)
May we acknowledge the mysterious will of God
especially in times of trouble;
and may we be generous toward others,
carrying the crosses that life brings
in our journey with Christ.
Lord, hear us.

4. For a desire to understand what is important
    in life.
(*pause*)
May we understand that God's ways are not
    our ways;
and may we be concerned for what is of lasting value
so that God's plan for each of us may be fulfilled,
bringing us happiness
in doing what God wants.
Lord, hear us.

Priest/Leader

Loving God,
you provide for us always.
Deepen our confidence in your love for us
and grant what we need
through Christ our Lord. Amen.

SUNDAY 23   YEAR A

Priest/Leader

"Where two or three are gathered in my name,
I am there with them."
We meet in the name of Jesus
and we have listened to God's word.
With renewed confidence, we turn to our God
for what we need.

1. For the courage to witness to our faith.
(*pause*)
May we have the courage to stand up
for what we believe,
correcting those who oppose the truth,
by lives that witness to the scripture
and values that reflect the commandments
        of God.
Lord, hear us.

2. For a desire to love one another.
(*pause*)
Paul sums up the commandments of God
in his teaching that we must love one another.
May we turn from sin in our lives,
eager to carry out the command of Jesus
that is at the heart of our faith.
Lord, hear us.

3. For peace in our families and communities.
(*pause*)
May the Lord's teaching
compel us to forgive one another
especially in family quarrels;
and may our desire to forgive one another
overcome the hurts we have experienced.
Lord, hear us.

4. For an awareness of Jesus' presence among us.
(*pause*)
May we acknowledge Jesus' presence
        among us
in the church and in the community;
and may his presence
be a source of strength for us
in discerning how we are to live.
Lord, hear us.

Priest/Leader

God of all consolation,
your Son is always with us.
May we be encouraged by his presence
and renewed in our confidence of your love.
We ask this through Christ our Lord.
        Amen.

Priest/Leader

"The Lord is merciful and gracious."
God's word has been broken for us
and its teaching nourishes our spirit.
Strengthened by that teaching,
we approach our God for what we need.

1. For the gift of gentleness.
(*pause*)
God commands us to avoid anger and
        resentment.
May we have the gift of gentleness toward others,
not returning evil for evil
but striving for that compassion and love
that we hope for from the Lord.
Lord, hear us.

2. For a sense of Christ's presence among us.
(*pause*)
May we be moved by a sense of Christ's presence.
By lives that reflect his teaching,
may we be his faithful disciples,
witnessing the love and compassion of Christ,
who is Lord of both living and dead.
Lord, hear us.

3. For a desire to forgive.
(*pause*)
Jesus commands us to forgive one another.
May we take his teaching with such seriousness
that we will truly live as his disciples,
eager to forgive those who hurt us
in our families and in our communities.
Lord, hear us.

4. For an understanding of God's generous love.
(*pause*)
The gospel teaches us that God's love is boundless
and God's forgiveness without limit.
May we grow in understanding God's love
so that we may be gentle with ourselves
and with others.
Lord, hear us.

Priest/Leader

God of compassion,
fill us with a sense of your love for us
and grant what we need.
We ask this through Christ our Lord. Amen.

SUNDAY 25   YEAR A

Priest/Leader

"The last will be first, and the first will be last."
We have heard God's word
and been strengthened by its teaching.
Now we turn to our loving God
for what we need
in the church and in the community.

1. For a sense of God's majesty.
(pause)
"So are my ways higher than your ways
and my thoughts than your thoughts."
May we be comforted by a sense of God's majesty,
consoled by God's forgiveness,
and open to God's purposes for us in life.
Lord, hear us.

2. For a desire to be pleasing to God.
(pause)
May we be anxious to please our God
by lives that reflect sound teaching;
and may we reject anything in life
that is unworthy of the gospel
so that Christ may be glorified in us.
Lord, hear us.

3. For a deeper understanding of God's gracious love.
(pause)
May the love of God increase in our hearts;
and may we be constantly comforted
by the immensity of the love of our God,
who teaches us not to live by the world's values
but to care for the least important in society.
Lord, hear us.

4. For an awareness of the compassion of our God.
(pause)
God does not judge by human standards
and God's gentleness is beyond our understanding.

May we learn to trust in the compassion of our God
and may we be generous toward others
as God is generous toward us.
Lord, hear us.

Priest/Leader

God of all mercies,
help us to be generous in your love.
Listen to our prayers for what we need.
We ask this through Christ our Lord. Amen.

SUNDAY 26   YEAR A

Priest/Leader

"Jesus Christ is Lord,
to the glory of God the Father."
We have been strengthened and nourished
by God's word, broken for us.
Encouraged by its teaching,
we turn to our God for what we need.

1. For a spirit of generosity.
(pause)
Our God is compassion and love,
eager to forgive when we repent of sin.
May we too be a people of forgiveness,
not holding grudges, but accepting people
when they turn to us in need.
Lord, hear us.

2. For an understanding of the majesty of Christ.
(pause)
Jesus emptied himself for us
and became a servant for our sake.
May we grow in understanding the heights
to which God raised him
and worship him as Lord of all.
Lord, hear us.

3. For a desire to live by the truth.
(pause)
May our yes be yes and our no be no;
and may we be people of the truth,
faithful in what we promise,
and witnessing to the gospel
in how we live.
Lord, hear us.

4. For a desire to witness to God's reign.
(*pause*)
The reign of God is mysteriously present among us
and no one is excluded
who tries to be faithful to God's way.
May we resist judging who is worthy of God's
    goodness
but rely on God's mercy on us all.
Lord, hear us.

Priest/Leader

God of mercy,
have pity on your children.
Teach us to forgive others as you forgive us.
We ask this through Christ our Lord. Amen.

SUNDAY 27   YEAR A

Priest/Leader

"The stone that the builders rejected has become the
    cornerstone."
God's word is powerful and disturbing.
Strengthened by its teaching,
we approach our God for what we need.

1. For the gift of gratitude to God.
(*pause*)
May we be a people of thankfulness—
aware of what God has done for us;
and may our gratitude to God
be reflected in our lives of concern
for other people.
Lord, hear us.

2. For the gift of peace.
(*pause*)
May we experience peace in our lives—
the peace that comes from listening to the gospel,
reflecting on its meaning,
and living by it's teaching
in mind and heart and deed.
Lord, hear us.

3. For the gift of producing good fruit.
(*pause*)
May our lives be fruitful in God's service,
and, in our living by the gospel teaching,

may God's purposes be fulfilled;
and may we share with others
the gifts that God has generously given us.
Lord, hear us.

4. For the gift of wisdom.
(*pause*)
The stone rejected by the builders became
    the cornerstone.
May we have the gift of wisdom
to discern the signs of the times;
and may we be open to what God wants
in the church and in the community.
Lord, hear us.

Priest/Leader

God of all consolation,
your truth sets us free,
your way leads to life.
Grant what we need, through Christ our Lord.
    Amen.

SUNDAY 28   YEAR A

Priest/Leader

"The Lord God will wipe away the tears from
    all faces."
The word of God consoles and comforts us.
Strengthened by its teaching,
we ask our God for what we need.

1. For a deeper understanding of God's love.
(*pause*)
God's saving purposes are for all the world.
May we grow in understanding God's love
that takes away the power of death
and promises consolation and hope
for people everywhere.
Lord, hear us.

2. For trust in God's goodness.
(*pause*)
Like Paul, we live through good times
    and bad,
times of poverty and times of plenty.
Like him, may we bless God always,
trusting God's concern for us

and generous in our care for others.
Lord, hear us.

3. For an openness to what God wants.
(*pause*)
May we be open to what God wants
and reach out to others in life
so that God's reign might be proclaimed
and people come to understand God's love
for all the people of the world.
Lord, hear us.

4. For a desire to live by the gospel.
(*pause*)
Jesus calls us to take seriously
the demands of the gospel.
May we be constant in reviewing what we value
    in life
and be witnesses to his teaching
by lives of integrity, honesty, and truth.
Lord, hear us.

Priest/Leader

God of our ancestors, may your kingdom
    come!
Keep us faithful to your ways
and grant what we need.
We ask this through Christ our Lord. Amen.

SUNDAY 29   YEAR A

Priest/Leader

"Give…to God the things that are God's."
The word of God
nourishes us in our journey through life.
We have listened to its teaching
and now turn to our God for what we need.

1. For an awareness that God is
    Lord of all.
(*pause*)
God is ruler of all the world—
past, present, and to come.
May we learn to trust in God's purposes,
confessing that, apart from God,
there is no meaning in life.
Lord, hear us.

2. For faith in action.
(*pause*)
Paul commended the Christian churches
for their faith in action.
May we too be the people of God
who take seriously the way of Christ
in how we live and what we value.
Lord, hear us.

3. For a right attitude toward God.
(*pause*)
May we honor our God in all of life
by what we say and what we do;
and may we be witnesses to the teaching
we have received
in what we consider of lasting value in life.
Lord, hear us.

4. For the gift of honesty.
(*pause*)
May we be people of the truth
and honest in all that we do;
and may we not be ashamed to let
    gospel values
influence our daily lives
of community and social concern.
Lord, hear us.

Priest/Leader

Lord God of the universe,
we worship you and thank you
for the gifts you give us.
Grant what we need
through Christ our Lord. Amen.

SUNDAY 30   YEAR A

Priest/Leader

"You shall love your neighbor as yourself."
God's powerful word
nourishes us in life's journey.
We have listened to its teaching
and now we turn to our God
for what we need.

1. For a desire to live justly.
(*pause*)

God's justice requires us to treat one another
with compassion and love.
May we be aware of others' needs
and may our response be marked always
by justice and integrity.
Lord, hear us.

2. For the gift of deep faith in God.
(pause)
Paul commends the churches
for the example they provide
in faith and joy.
May we too deepen our faith in our God,
living as God's servants in God's world.
Lord, hear us.

3. For the gift of love.
(pause)
The greatest commandment is to love God
and to love our neighbor.
May we be known as a community of love:
a people whose love for God
is lived out in caring for one another.
Lord, hear us.

4. For the gift of service.
(pause)
We are commanded to love
our neighbor as ourselves.
May we learn from the Law and the Prophets
to be generous in the service
of God and of one another.
Lord, hear us.

Priest/Leader

Generous God,
you give us all that we need
in the church and in the community.
Help us to be your true servants.
We ask this through Christ our Lord. Amen.

SUNDAY 31   YEAR A

Priest/Leader

"The greatest among you
will be your servant."

God's word nourishes us by its teaching.
Strengthened by that word,
we turn to our God for what we need.

1. For leaders in the churches.
(pause)
May all who exercise leadership
in the churches
be people of integrity and justice.
May they be faithful teachers of God's good news
and honest in practicing what they preach.
Lord, hear us.

2. For a desire to spread the good news.
(pause)
May we be eager to pass on the good news
about God's love and God's way.
May our enthusiasm for the gospel
be reflected not simply in what we proclaim
but in what we value and how we live.
Lord, hear us.

3. For a spirit of compassion.
(pause)
May the good news by which we live
move us to compassion for others;
and may the teaching of the gospel
never be a source of oppression
but of freedom to live as children of God.
Lord, hear us.

4. For a spirit of humility.
(pause)
May we understand our worth in God's sight
and rejoice that we are the children of God.
And may we be faithful disciples of Jesus,
following his example and his teaching
to be servants in the community.
Lord, hear us.

Priest/Leader

God of consolation,
you sent your Son Jesus
to be the servant of all.
Teach us to imitate him
in our care for one another.
We ask this through Christ our Lord.
    Amen.

Priest/Leader

"You know neither the day nor the hour."
God's word challenges us to stay awake.
Strengthened by its teaching,
we turn with confidence to our God
for what we need.

1. For the gift of wisdom.
(pause)
God's wisdom is God's plan for all people,
a gift of light that never grows dim.
May we always look for the wisdom of God
so that we know what is of lasting value in life
and lead lives that accord with God's will.
Lord, hear us.

2. For trust in God's goodness.
(pause)
We commend to our God
those who have fallen asleep in the Lord.
We confess our faith in God's power to save,
confident that God will care for us
in life and in death.
Lord, hear us.

3. For the grace to be ready when the
        Lord comes.
(pause)
When the Lord visits,
may we be ready to respond in love.
May we care with love for those in need,
recognizing the Lord's presence
in those who are suffering in our world.
Lord, hear us.

4. For a serious desire to follow Christ.
(pause)
Like the wise women in the gospel story,
may we be ready to greet the Lord at all times.
May we take seriously the teaching of Jesus
by lives that proclaim gospel values
and actions that witness to his way.
Lord, hear us.

Priest/Leader

God of the promises,
you never leave your people.
Comfort and strengthen us in times of trouble
and grant what we need
through Christ our Lord. Amen.

Priest/Leader

"Well done, good and trustworthy slave."
God's word, broken for us,
comforts and encourages us in life's journey.
Strengthened by its teaching,
we turn to our God
for what we need.

1. For generosity of spirit.
(pause)
Like the wise woman of the scripture,
may we be generous in God's service,
alert to the needs of others in the community,
and eager to share with them
the gifts we have received from God.
Lord, hear us.

2. For an openness to God in our lives.
(pause)
Paul teaches us to watch for the Day of
        the Lord,
who comes like a thief in the night.
May we be alert to God's presence in our lives,
looking for ways to be of service
as children of the light.
Lord, hear us.

3. For a desire to be God's faithful people.
(pause)
We acknowledge that God has called us
to lives of faithful service.
May we strive always to live by the gospel,
using God's gifts wisely
in the church and in the community.
Lord, hear us.

4. For a right attitude in our approach to God.
(*pause*)
May our approach to God be one of love
and not of fear;
and in serving God and our neighbor
may God's love spur us on
to do what is right in God's sight.
Lord, hear us.

Priest/Leader

God of all consolation,
you reveal yourself to us as a God of love.
Help us respond to you in love
and grant what we need.
We ask this through Christ our Lord. Amen.

FEAST OF CHRIST THE KING YEAR A

Priest/Leader

"He must reign until he has put all his enemies
        under his feet."
On this celebration of Christ the King
we have been nourished by God's word
and we turn to our Lord with confidence
for what we need.

1. For a deeper faith in God's love for us.
(*pause*)
God is our shepherd
who desires to gather the lost
and whose concern is for the weakest of the flock.
May we deepen our faith in God's love for us
and rejoice that God cares for each one of us.
Lord, hear us.

2. For trust in God's power to save.
(*pause*)
Jesus has been raised from the dead,
the firstfruits of those who have fallen asleep.
May we always rejoice in the Lordship
        of Christ,
trusting in God's power
to save us from sin and death.
Lord, hear us.

3. For a desire to serve Christ our King.
(*pause*)

May we be faithful servants of our King,
living lives that reflect the values of his reign,
reaching out to those in need
and caring for them in the church
and in the community.
Lord, hear us.

4. For a desire to be kingdom people.
(*pause*)
Christ the King is our ruler—
he proclaims justice, love, and peace.
May these be the marks of God's people;
and may we desire to live by the gospel
so that God's reign may come in our world.
Lord, hear us.

Priest/Leader

Almighty God, ruler of the universe,
we worship you and honor your name.
Grant what we need to be faithful servants
of Jesus our brother,
for he is Lord, forever and ever. Amen.

SUNDAY 2   YEAR B

Priest/Leader

"Speak, LORD, for your servant is listening."
God's word has been spoken to us
and, like Samuel, we must listen to its message.
We now turn to the God of our ancestors
for what we need in the church and in
        the community.

1. For an openness to the call of God.
(*pause*)
The story of Samuel teaches us
to be open to God's call in life.
May we be alert to the needs of the times,
revealed in scripture, in the church,
and in the life of the community.
Lord, hear us.

2. For a right attitude to our bodies.
(*pause*)
Paul commands us to care for our bodies,
acknowledging them as a gift of God.
May we not abuse or despise our bodies

but treat them with respect and moderation
as temples of God's Holy Spirit.
Lord, hear us.

3. For a desire to be disciples of Christ.
(*pause*)
Jesus calls people to follow him.
Like the first disciples, Andrew and Peter,
may we be faithful followers of our Lord,
attentive to his teaching
and living according to the gospel.
Lord, hear us.

4. For a desire to teach others the way of Christ.
(*pause*)
May we be faithful teachers of others
in the ways of faith,
passing on the message of Jesus
about what is important in life
by what we value and how we live.
Lord, hear us.

Priest/Leader

God of the promises,
you sent Jesus, your Son,
to be our teacher and guide.
Help us to be faithful disciples
and followers of his way.
We ask this through Christ our Lord.
     Amen.

SUNDAY 3   YEAR B

Priest/Leader

"Repent, and believe in the good news."
This is the first teaching of the Christ.
Nourished by his word broken for us,
we turn to our God
for what we need in the church and in the
        community.

1. For the gift of repentance.
(*pause*)
The people of Nineveh responded to the preaching
    of Jonah,
turning from their sins
and choosing the way of the Lord.

May we too be conscious of the power of sin in
        our lives
and refuse to be controlled by it.
Lord, hear us.

2. For an appreciation of what is of value in life.
(*pause*)
Paul teaches us about the shortness of life
and urges us to make serious choices
because our world is passing away.
May we learn to appreciate what is of lasting value
        in life
and lead lives that are acceptable to God.
Lord, hear us.

3. For an awareness of the cost of discipleship.
(*pause*)
The good news of Jesus calls us to repentance,
threatening power and status
in church and society.
May we acknowledge the cost of discipleship
and support one another in living by the gospel.
Lord, hear us.

4. For a desire to follow the Christ.
(*pause*)
Like the first disciples,
may we be open to the call of Christ,
eager to be his followers.
By our lifestyle and values
may others come to know the purposes of God.
Lord, hear us.

Priest/Leader

God of all consolation,
you command us to follow your Son.
Help us be good disciples
in what we do and what we teach.
We ask this through Christ our Lord. Amen.

SUNDAY 4   YEAR B

Priest/Leader

Jesus taught with authority—
and we have listened to his teaching.
Strengthened in faith by its message,
we ask our God for what we need.

1. For prophets in our world.
(*pause*)
May we be alert to the prophets in
       our world—
in the church and in the community—
and may we be open to their teaching
about God's purposes
for the church and society.
Lord, hear us.

2. For a sense of balance in life.
(*pause*)
Paul teaches us to be careful in what we do,
finding time for God in the busyness of life.
May we be attentive to the needs of others,
eager to show our love for God
in our concern for those we care for.
Lord, hear us.

3. For a desire to live by the gospel.
(*pause*)
May we be faithful to the teaching of
       the gospel,
proclaiming it as God's word for our time;
and may our lives and values
witness to its authority
and its power to transform people
       and society.
Lord, hear us.

4. For an appreciation of Jesus the teacher.
(*pause*)
May we look to the Lord Jesus
who taught the people with authority,
bringing them hope and healing;
and may his teaching strengthen us
in times of trouble and need.
Lord, hear us.

Priest/Leader

God, the source of all good things,
we thank you for Christ the good teacher.
Help us to be faithful to his message
and grant what we need
through Christ our Lord. Amen.

Priest/Leader

Jesus came to preach the good news.
God's word has been broken for us
and we are strengthened by its message.
We ask our God to look kindly on us
and to grant us what we need.

1. For a sense of purpose in life.
(*pause*)
May we not, like Job,
be overcome by despair about life.
Rather, may we acknowledge
God's purposes for our world
and for each of us.
Lord, hear us.

2. For a desire to spread the gospel.
(*pause*)
Like Paul, may we be enthusiastic about the gospel,
living by its teaching and witnessing to its values
so that people everywhere may know the
       good news
and find freedom and fulfillment
in all that they do.
Lord, hear us.

3. For a desire to be of service.
(*pause*)
May we take Jesus as our model in life,
and by our concern for others—
especially those who are sick or in need—
witness to his teaching in the church
and in the community.
Lord, hear us.

4. For a sense of balance in life.
(*pause*)
May we look for time to be alone with our God,
seeking God's will through prayer and silence
so that our daily lives may not be empty
but filled with a sense of God's presence
and a desire to live as God commands.
Lord, hear us.

Priest/Leader

God of the promises,
you fill us with joy in your presence.
Grant what we need in the church
and in the community.
We ask this through Christ our Lord. Amen.

SUNDAY 6   YEAR B

Priest/Leader

"Be made clean!"
Jesus' word of healing to the leper
brings consolation to all of us.
Encouraged by that word,
we ask our God for what we need.

1. For those on the margins of society.
(pause)
We pray for those whom society rejects,
especially in our country and community.
May we be people of compassion
reaching out to those
whom society abandons.
Lord, hear us.

2. For a desire to imitate Christ.
(pause)
May we be followers of Jesus
in how we live,
careful to avoid hurting others
by attitudes that discriminate
and language that offends.
Lord, hear us.

3. For a desire to be healers in society.
(pause)
Jesus is our model
of acceptance, of tolerance, and of healing.
Like him, may we be healers in society,
accepting people who are different from ourselves
in language, culture, and faith.
Lord, hear us.

4. For a desire to spread the good news.
(pause)
All of us experience the healing love of God
expressed in the care and concern of others.

By what we profess and how we live,
may we declare to others our faith in the good news
of God's love and acceptance for all peoples.
Lord, hear us.

Priest/Leader

God of all people,
you bring healing and wholeness to all the world.
Listen to our prayers and grant what we need
through Christ our Lord. Amen.

SUNDAY 7   YEAR B

Priest/Leader

"We have never seen anything like this!"
We share the joy of those
who experienced the healing forgiveness of God
     in Christ.
Strengthened in faith, we approach our God
for what we need.

1. For joy that our sins are forgiven.
(pause)
God declares our sins are forgiven,
refusing to recall our deeds in the past.
May our joy in experiencing God's forgiveness
encourage us to avoid sin in our lives
and to live by the commandments.
Lord, hear us.

2. For joy that we have been chosen in Christ.
(pause)
We rejoice that God's yes in Christ
includes all of us who have been baptized in him.
May we be accepting of others,
unselfish in our attitude to them
as God is unselfish toward us.
Lord, hear us.

3. For joy in the gift of forgiveness.
(pause)
As we have been forgiven by God
may we be forgiving toward others;
not bearing grudges for past mistakes
and generous, like God, in forgiving offenses
in our families and communities.
Lord, hear us.

4. For joy in God's power to save.
(*pause*)
Like the people in the gospel story,
may we rejoice in God's gift
of wholeness and healing;
and may we bring that healing to others
by our forgiveness and acceptance of them.
Lord, hear us.

Priest/Leader

God of mercy,
have pity on all your children.
Keep us faithful to the way of Christ
and grant what we need.
We ask this through Christ our Lord. Amen.

SUNDAY 8   YEAR B

Priest/Leader

"One puts new wine into fresh wineskins."
God's word is always new for us,
refreshing us with its message
and calling us to new responses in life.
Comforted by this word,
we turn to our God for what we need.

1. For integrity in our lives.
(*pause*)
God's love for the people
is intense and everlasting.
May our response to that love
be reflected in lives of integrity and justice,
with a special care for the poor in our world.
Lord, hear us.

2. For confidence in living by the gospel.
(*pause*)
God's love for us
is renewed in every generation.
May we be faithful disciples of Jesus,
confident that God's Spirit
gives us the strength to witness to the gospel.
Lord, hear us.

3. For an openness to what God wants.
(*pause*)
May we always be certain of God's love,

not afraid for the future
but open to new understandings of the gospel
and how we are to live
as followers of the Christ.
Lord, hear us.

4. For tolerance and patience in life.
(*pause*)
May we be tolerant of one another
in the church and in society,
acknowledging that God alone knows all truth;
and may we be patient in seeking to discern
the purposes of God.
Lord, hear us.

Priest/Leader

God of the promises,
you console us with your love.
Grant what we need
in the church and in society.
We ask this through Christ our Lord. Amen.

SUNDAY 9   YEAR B

Priest/Leader

"The Son of man is lord even of the sabbath."
God's word has been broken for us
and its good news comforts us in life.
Strengthened by its teaching,
we turn to our God
for what we need.

1. For a sense of balance in our lives.
(*pause*)
God commands us to keep the Sabbath
as a time dedicated to the Lord.
May we learn to keep a balance in our lives,
acknowledging the need for rest, quiet, and
    refreshment
for ourselves, our families, and our world.
Lord, hear us.

2. For a sense of God's protection.
(*pause*)
Paul teaches us that God's power is at work in us
like a light shining out of the darkness.
May this teaching comfort and strengthen us,

encouraging us to proclaim gospel values
even at the cost of rejection and suffering.
Lord, hear us.

3. For a right attitude to the Lord's Day.
(*pause*)
May we acknowledge God's presence
and purpose in our world,
taking time for prayer and worship and
    recreation;
and by our celebration of the Lord's Day,
may we witness to what is of lasting value
    in life.
Lord, hear us.

4. For a desire to be of service to others.
(*pause*)
The Sabbath is the Lord's and ours too,
a time for reflection and renewal.
May our worship of God and the faith we profess
be lived in our care for others
in the church and in the community.
Lord, hear us.

Priest/Leader

Lord God of the Sabbath,
we bless you and thank you for your gift of rest.
Grant what we need to be good servants of
    your Son.
For he is Lord, forever and ever. Amen.

SUNDAY 10   YEAR B

Priest/Leader

"Whoever does the will of God
is my brother and sister and mother."
Strengthened by God's word,
we are confident in bringing before the Lord
our needs and those of all God's people.

1. For confidence that God's goodness overcomes
    all evil.
(*pause*)
Even from the beginning, after the Fall
when sin entered our world,
God promised that evil would be crushed.
We ask for confidence in God's power

to fulfill all that has been promised.
Lord, hear us.

2. For a sense of hope in the future.
(*pause*)
The future is known to God alone;
and those who are faithful
are promised a home that lasts forever.
May we be confident of God's love and God's
    purposes
now and in the future.
Lord, hear us.

3. For unity of purpose among God's people.
(*pause*)
A divided household cannot be strong.
We pray for unity of purpose
among the people of God,
witnessing to what the gospel demands
and faithful in proclaiming the teaching of Jesus.
Lord, hear us.

4. For a desire to do God's will.
(*pause*)
Those who belong to God's family
are committed to doing God's will.
May our faithfulness in living the gospel
make us worthy to be called
brothers and sisters of Jesus.
Lord, hear us.

Priest/Leader

God of our ancestors,
you call us to be your people
in every generation.
Listen in love to our prayers
and grant what we need,
in Jesus' name. Amen.

SUNDAY 11   YEAR B

Priest/Leader

"I the LORD have spoken;
I will accomplish it."
God's word is at work in our world
as we come to the Lord with confidence
for all our needs in the church and in the world.

1. For an acceptance of God's purposes.
(*pause*)
In the providence of God,
the weak become strong
and the strong weak.
We ask for a sense of God's majesty
and the courage to let God rule in our lives.
Lord, hear us.

2. For a desire to live by the gospel.
(*pause*)
Whether we are alive or dead,
we must be intent on pleasing God.
May our lives be based on gospel teaching
so that we may give faithful witness
in the law courts of Christ.
Lord, hear us.

3. For insight into the mystery of God's reign.
(*pause*)
The reign of God is hidden, mysterious, and effective.
May we welcome God's purposes for our lives
and, by witnessing to gospel values,
become the harvest planned by God
for the saving of the world.
Lord, hear us.

4. For an attitude of welcome in the community.
(*pause*)
The reign of God excludes no one;
and all find shelter in God's presence.
May we too be a people of welcome
in the church and in the community,
living signs of God's hospitality and love.
Lord, hear us.

Priest/Leader

Lord, may your kingdom come!
Teach us to be generous disciples
and grant what we need
through Christ our Lord. Amen.

SUNDAY 12   YEAR B

Priest/Leader

"Who then is this, that even the wind and the sea
    obey him?"

With the confidence that comes
from belonging to God's family,
we bring before the Lord
our needs and those of all the people of the world.

1. For a deeper awareness of the majesty of God.
(*pause*)
God is Lord of earth and sky and sea.
May we grow in understanding God's
        greatness
in our complex universe,
and still be confident
in the presence of our God.
Lord, hear us.

2. For an understanding of the love of Christ.
(*pause*)
The love of Christ overwhelms us
and compels us to lives of service.
As faithful disciples of the gospel,
may our lives bear witness
to the new creation he has begun.
Lord, hear us.

3. For a deeper faith in Christ.
(*pause*)
When we feel afraid or threatened
by forces and fears
that are greater than we can bear,
may we be filled with faith in Christ
and be comforted by his power to rescue us.
Lord, hear us.

4. For courage to trust in God's love.
(*pause*)
In times of great stress and sorrow
—from sickness, loss,
and the death of those we love—
may we turn to our God
and find the consolation that we desire.
Lord, hear us.

Priest/Leader

God of consolation,
be near to us in our time of need.
Remind us of your constant love
and grant what we ask.
We ask this through Christ our Lord. Amen.

Priest/Leader

"Go in peace, and be healed of your disease."
Encouraged by the compassion of Jesus
toward those in pain,
we turn to the Lord
for what we need.

1. For an appreciation of life as a gift from God.
(pause)
Since we are made in God's image,
may we thank our God always for the gift
    of life;
and may we care for everything that God
    has made,
avoiding what destroys our world
by what we do and how we live.
Lord, hear us.

2. For the gift of generous love.
(pause)
The Lord Jesus was rich but became poor for our
    sakes.
May we who live in comfort
be aware of others in need
and imitate the love of Christ
by lives of charity and care.
Lord, hear us.

3. For an appreciation of God's inclusive love.
(pause)
Jesus taught us by his example
to welcome those whom society rejected.
May we be alert in the church and community
to people who feel excluded,
and look for ways to welcome them
    with love.
Lord, hear us.

4. For healing in our lives.
(pause)
May all who are broken or bereaved,
alone or in sorrow
be comforted by the compassion of Jesus
and the care of those in the community
called the church.
Lord, hear us.

Priest/Leader

God of life and love,
fill us with compassion for those in need,
and grant what we ask
through Christ our Lord. Amen.

Priest/Leader

"My grace is sufficient for you,"
says the Lord.
We have been nourished by God's word
and we turn to the Lord in our need
for ourselves, our church, and our world.

1. For the gift to accept prophets among us.
(pause)
Like the people of Israel,
may we look to the prophets God sends,
in the church and in the world,
to remind us of the teachings of scripture
and the commandments of God.
Lord, hear us.

2. For an acceptance of God's providence in life.
(pause)
In all our needs
—and especially in the times of trouble,
sickness, and bereavement—
may we be strengthened by the love of God,
who cares for us even in our weakness.
Lord, hear us.

3. For a renewed eagerness to follow Christ.
(pause)
May we be moved to follow the way of Jesus,
confessing him as the prophet of God
and the bearer of God's wisdom;
and may we be eager disciples of his teaching
in how we live and what we proclaim.
Lord, hear us.

4. For the gift of great faith.
(pause)
May we learn to trust the Lord
and be strong in faith.
May our lives bear witness

to the teaching of the gospel
in our homes and in our communities.
Lord, hear us.

Priest/Leader

God of consolation, strengthen the faith of your
    people.
Alert us to the prophets in our midst
and show us your will
for the church and for the world.
We ask this through Christ our Lord. Amen.

SUNDAY 15   YEAR B

Priest/Leader

We are claimed as God's own people,
chosen from the beginning.
Nourished by God's word,
we turn to our God in prayer
for ourselves and all God's people.

1. For the gift to accept prophets among us.
(pause)
God sends us prophets and teachers
to remind us of the commandments
and the way that leads to life.
May we accept the prophets God sends,
calling us to lives of justice and truth.
Lord, hear us.

2. For an awareness of God's generous love.
(pause)
We are a people chosen by God
before the world began.
May we be conscious of God's generous love
revealed to us in Christ
that brings forgiveness of sin and abundance
    of life.
Lord, hear us.

3. For a sense of our mission in life.
(pause)
Like the Twelve who were sent to spread the
    good news,
may we recognize that we also share their mission
of teaching and witnessing
to the truth of God

revealed in Jesus.
Lord, hear us.

4. For a sense of urgency in living the gospel.
(pause)
May we resist the attraction of wealth and
    possessions,
but be people of integrity and compassion,
generous in our caring for one another
and eager to live
by the teaching of the gospel.
Lord, hear us.

Priest/Leader

God of the promises,
teach us to be content with what we have
and to trust in your merciful love.
We ask this through Christ our Lord.
    Amen.

SUNDAY 16   YEAR B

Priest/Leader

"He is our peace;
in his flesh he has made both groups
    into one."
Strengthened by God's word,
we come to our living God
with what we need
for ourselves, our church, and our world.

1. For shepherds and leaders of God's people.
(pause)
We pray for those who are leaders among
    God's people
that they may be faithful to the teaching of the
    scripture,
people of integrity and honesty,
and alert to the promptings
of God's Spirit.
Lord, hear us.

2. For peace in our world.
(pause)
In Christ, we have become one people of God.
May we strive for unity among all peoples,
working for peace in the community

by attitudes of acceptance and tolerance
that reflect the teaching of the gospel.
Lord, hear us.

3. For a desire to find time for God.
(*pause*)
Like the apostles, we too are commanded
    by Jesus
to come away and rest awhile,
to find time for God in prayer and quiet times.
May we relish the time we spend with God
and be strengthened by those times of rest.
Lord, hear us.

4. For those who are searching for the truth.
(*pause*)
We pray for those like sheep without shepherds
who are searching for the truth
about life, about God, about reality.
May they find meaning in the teaching of
    the gospel
and find peace and joy in living the way of Christ.
Lord, hear us.

Priest/Leader

God of all peoples,
you are our shepherd
and you care for us always.
Hear the prayers we have made and grant them,
    we pray,
through Christ our Lord. Amen.

SUNDAY 17   YEAR B

Priest/Leader

"There is…one Lord, one faith,
one baptism, one God
and Father of all."
With confidence in God's love
we bring before the Lord
our needs in the church and in the world.

1. For confidence in God's providence.
(*pause*)
Like the prophet Elisha,
may we be conscious of God's goodness to us
in providing food and shelter.

And may we be moved to be generous
to those who need our help.
Lord, hear us.

2. For an attitude of acceptance of others.
(*pause*)
Moved by the Spirit of God, we are commanded
to be charitable, selfless, gentle, and patient.
May we work together for unity and peace
in our homes
and in our communities.
Lord, hear us.

3. For an awareness of our need for God.
(*pause*)
Like the crowds who followed Jesus,
hungry for his teaching and his care,
may we be open to the nourishment he offers
in the breaking of the word
and the breaking of the Eucharist.
Lord, hear us.

4. For a spirit of generosity toward others.
(*pause*)
Jesus fed the crowds with five loaves and two fish.
May we be generous in sharing what we have
so that people may come to acknowledge
the generous love of God
for all the world.
Lord, hear us.

Priest/Leader

God of love,
you created the world and all it holds.
Teach us to take care of the world
and to share its riches.
We ask this through Christ our Lord. Amen.

SUNDAY 18   YEAR B

Priest/Leader

"Whoever comes to me will never be hungry,
and whoever believes in me will never be thirsty."
Nourished and strengthened by God's word,
we approach the Lord with confidence,
bringing our needs and the needs of people
    everywhere.

1. For a spirit of thanksgiving for God's gifts.
(pause)
May we learn to appreciate God's gifts to us
and to develop an attitude of thanksgiving,
acknowledging the fruitfulness of the earth
and renewing our commitment
to care for God's creation.
Lord, hear us.

2. For a sense of spiritual renewal.
(pause)
We are commanded to put aside our old self
and to be renewed spiritually.
May we be open to God's Spirit,
seeking to be faithful to the way of Christ,
living lives of holiness and goodness
        and truth.
Lord, hear us.

3. For a deeper faith in Jesus.
(pause)
We confess Jesus as the One sent by God.
May we grow in faith,
accepting his way as God's way
and his teaching as food
that nourishes us in our journey through life.
Lord, hear us.

4. For a desire to share the bread of life.
(pause)
Jesus is the bread that gives life to the world.
By our obedience to him and his
        commandments,
may we bring others to faith
so that they may share the bread
that gives life to the world.
Lord, hear us.

Priest/Leader

Creator God,
we thank you for the gift of your Son—
Jesus the giver of life.
Increase our faith in him
and grant the prayers we ask
through Christ our Lord. Amen.

Priest/Leader

"Whoever eats of this bread will live forever."
We have been fed with the bread that is
        God's word
and we now present to the Lord
our prayers for the church and for the world.

1. For confidence in God's caring.
(pause)
God sent an angel to provide food for Elijah.
May we be confident of God's generous
        love for us
in our journey through life;
and may we, in turn,
provide for the hungry in our world.
Lord, hear us.

2. For the gift of forgiveness.
(pause)
We are to forgive one another
as God forgave us in Christ.
May we be tolerant and graceful
in our dealings with one another,
as children whom God loves.
Lord, hear us.

3. For faith in God's promises.
(pause)
Jesus is the bread of life
and his teaching is the promise of everlasting life.
May we be faithful to that teaching
that we may be raised to fullness of life
on the last day.
Lord, hear us.

4. For a desire to be faithful witnesses.
(pause)
We believe that Jesus is the bread of life
given for the life of the world.
May we be his faithful witnesses,
confessing that he is the wisdom of God
and living according to his teaching.
Lord, hear us.

Priest/Leader

Creator God of all the world,
we confess your Son Jesus
as living bread from heaven.
Listen to the prayers we make
through Christ our Lord. Amen.

SUNDAY 20   YEAR B

Priest/Leader

"Whoever eats of this bread will live forever."
We have listened to God's word
and been nourished by its teaching.
We now turn to the Lord with confidence,
asking what we need
for ourselves, our community, and our world.

1. For the gift of wisdom.
(pause)
Wisdom is God's gift of discernment,
teaching us to know what is right
and pleasing to the Lord our God.
May we seek to live by the wisdom of God,
walking always in the way of the Lord.
Lord, hear us.

2. For simplicity in our lives.
(pause)
May we learn to be content with what we have,
acknowledging the Lord
as the giver of all good things,
and constantly giving thanks to God
for the blessings we have in life.
Lord, hear us.

3. For an understanding of Jesus, the bread of life.
(pause)
Jesus has promised life forever
to those who eat his flesh and drink his blood.
May our sharing in this Eucharist
be a sign of our deeper commitment
to follow his teaching.
Lord, hear us.

4. For a desire to live for Christ.
(pause)
Life is God's gift to us; life is Christ's promise to us.

May our belonging to this community
and our celebration of this Eucharist
be a sign of our desire
to live for Christ forever.
Lord, hear us.

Priest/Leader

God of our ancestors,
all life comes from you.
Listen to our prayers this day.
We ask this through Christ our Lord. Amen.

SUNDAY 21   YEAR B

Priest/Leader

"You have the words of eternal life."
We have been strengthened by God's word
broken for us;
and now we turn to the Lord in faith,
asking for all our needs.

1. For a desire to serve God in the world.
(pause)
Like the people of Israel,
we have chosen to serve the Lord our God.
May we be good servants of God,
witnesses to God's teaching
about how we are to live.
Lord, hear us.

2. For those in our community who are married.
(pause)
Married Christians are commanded
to give way to one another in obedience to Christ.
May wives and husbands in our community
grow in forgiveness and love
as they witness to Christ in their lives.
Lord, hear us.

3. For perseverance in faith.
(pause)
May we be strong in faith,
choosing to follow the Lord
even when his teaching is difficult,
and confessing him always
as the Holy One of God.
Lord, hear us.

4. For a deeper understanding of the Eucharist.
(*pause*)
May we who celebrate the Eucharist
deepen our understanding
of what God has done for us in Christ;
and when we gather, may we be nourished
by the broken word and the broken bread.
Lord, hear us.

Priest/Leader

God of all consolation,
you gather your people to teach them your ways
and to remind them of your mighty deeds.
With confidence, we ask you to hear our prayers
through Christ our Lord. Amen.

SUNDAY 22   YEAR B

Priest/Leader

"Listen to me…and understand."
God's word has been broken for us
and we have been fed by its message
that brings eternal life.
With confidence we turn to our God
for the needs of the church and the world.

1. For a desire to follow God's commandments.
(*pause*)
Like the people of Israel,
may we be faithful in following God's ways
and constant in practicing charity and justice
so that others may be drawn to the truth of God
that leads to life.
Lord, hear us.

2. For the will to live as children of God.
(*pause*)
We have become God's children
by God's own choice.
May we be fruitful children in God's eyes,
caring for one another in the community
and in the church.
Lord, hear us.

3. For a commitment to the way of Jesus.
(*pause*)
May we be true followers of Jesus

who taught that religion is not
about human regulations
but about God's command
to live justly and graciously from our hearts.
Lord, hear us.

4. For a desire to keep ourselves true to
    the gospel.
(*pause*)
May we be guided by the gospel of Jesus,
living out its teaching
and worshiping God in faith
by what we value
and what we consider important in life.
Lord, hear us.

Priest/Leader

God of all goodness,
you command us to be constant in following
    the gospel.
Make us strong in faith
and grant what we ask
through Christ our Lord. Amen.

SUNDAY 23   YEAR B

Priest/Leader

"He has done everything well;
he even makes the deaf hear and the mute
    to speak."
We have been strengthened by God's word
and professed our faith.
Now we turn to our God with confidence
for our needs and those of all peoples.

1. For the gift of hope in God's promises.
(*pause*)
Isaiah commands us to have courage
and not to be afraid.
May we be aware of God's power
in our lives and in our world
and be renewed in hope to live as God wants.
Lord, hear us.

2. For an awareness of God's choices.
(*pause*)
God chooses the weak to confuse the strong

and makes them the inheritors of the
    kingdom.
May we become worthy children of our God,
becoming poor in God's sight
so that we may be rich in faith.
Lord, hear us.

3. For an openness to God's teaching.
(*pause*)
Like the man whom Jesus cured,
may our ears be open to hear God's word
and alert to the promptings of the Spirit
that we may be faithful in living
according to the gospel.
Lord, hear us.

4. For a desire to spread the good news.
(*pause*)
May we learn to speak clearly
the good news about Jesus Christ,
speaking openly and confidently
about what we believe
and how God wants us to live.
Lord, hear us.

Priest/Leader

God of all consolation,
you make us whole
by the preaching of the gospel.
May we bring that wholeness to all
    we meet
through Christ our Lord. Amen.

SUNDAY 24   YEAR B

Priest/Leader

"It is the Lord GOD who helps me;
who will declare me guilty?"
Nourished by the word of God,
we bring before the Lord
the needs of the church and the world.

1. For hope in the midst of suffering.
(*pause*)
Like the servants of God in every age
who suffer because of their faith,
may we be of good courage in suffering

and learn to trust in God's goodness
and the support of people of good will.
Lord, hear us.

2. For a desire to please God.
(*pause*)
Faith without deeds is dead.
May we show forth our faith in God
and be found pleasing to the Lord
by our care for those in need
in the church and in the community.
Lord, hear us.

3. For faith in Jesus as the Christ.
(*pause*)
Like Peter, may we confess Jesus as the Christ,
God's chosen one, the Savior;
and like Peter, may we learn to trust our God
whose ways are not our ways
and whose purposes are beyond our
    understanding.
Lord, hear us.

4. For an acceptance of the cross in our lives.
(*pause*)
May we learn from the example of Jesus
the cost of being a disciple;
and may we carry the crosses of life,
giving ourselves for others,
for the sake of the gospel.
Lord, hear us.

Priest/Leader

God of all consolation,
be with those who are suffering.
Give them courage to carry their cross,
and give us the strength to help them.
We ask this through Christ our Lord. Amen.

SUNDAY 25   YEAR B

Priest/Leader

"Whoever welcomes me," said Jesus,
"welcomes not me but the one who sent me."
We have been nourished by God's word
and now we turn to the Lord
for what we need to be a faithful people.

1. For the gift of perseverance.
(pause)
May we be constant in turning from evil
and holding to what is good.
May we have the grace of perseverance,
resisting those who would lead us into sin
and putting our trust in God.
Lord, hear us.

2. For those who bring peace to the world.
(pause)
May we be people of peace,
avoiding jealousy and ambition
in our families and in our communities;
and may we support by word and action
those who work for peace in our world.
Lord, hear us.

3. For a desire to be of service in the
        community.
(pause)
God has called us to be servants rather
        than masters.
May we learn to follow the example of Jesus,
who commanded us to welcome
the least important in the community
and minister to them.
Lord, hear us.

4. For an acceptance of the purposes of God
        for us.
(pause)
The way of Christ is the way of the cross.
May we accept that way
as the cost of discipleship,
ready to witness to gospel teaching
in how we live and what we value.
Lord, hear us.

Priest/Leader

Creator God, your Son died for us
and rose to bring us wholeness and healing.
May we be worthy disciples of Jesus
in his life of service.
We ask this through Christ our Lord.
        Amen.

Priest/Leader

"Whoever is not against us is for us."
We have listened to God's word, broken for us,
and professed our faith in God.
As God's people we reflect on our needs
and the needs of all the world.

1. For those who are prophets in the world.
(pause)
May we be guided by God's Spirit
to recognize those in the world
who speak the truth
and acknowledge that God's choices
are not limited by our expectations.
Lord, hear us.

2. For a right attitude toward wealth.
(pause)
James teaches us to be careful about wealth.
May our richness be measured
by our concern for justice,
and our wealth reckoned
by our concern for the poor.
Lord, hear us.

3. For those who are prophets in the church.
(pause)
May we always be open to prophecy
in our community and in our church,
welcoming those who remind us of
        gospel values,
calling us to service and generosity
in the name of Jesus.
Lord, hear us.

4. For a desire to take the gospel seriously.
(pause)
Jesus teaches us about the demands made
of those called to be his followers.
May we reflect on the seriousness of our call,
avoiding scandal to others in the church
and encouraging them by our faithfulness to the
        gospel.
Lord, hear us.

Priest/Leader

God of all ages,
you are with your people forever.
Teach us to be faithful followers of your Son
in all we do and say.
We ask this through Christ our Lord. Amen.

SUNDAY 27   YEAR B

Priest/Leader

"Whoever does not receive the kingdom of God
as a little child will never enter it."
We have listened to God's word
and now we open our hearts to the Lord,
recalling our needs.

1. For those who are our helpers in life.
(pause)
God created our first parents
in a partnership of loving service.
May we respect those whom God sends
as our partners in life
and as living signs of God's covenant of love.
Lord, hear us.

2. For those who are suffering or in need.
(pause)
Through his suffering, Jesus has entered his glory.
May we who are his sisters and brothers
persevere in hope,
comforting those who are in need
by our patience, our care, and our love.
Lord, hear us.

3. For a childlike attitude toward God's reign.
(pause)
May we be like children in welcoming God's reign
—full of joy and anticipation—
eager to do what God wants
and filled with trust
in God's loving purposes for us all.
Lord, hear us.

4. For an awareness of the demands of the gospel.
(pause)
Jesus' teaching about divorce
reminds us of the demands of the gospel.

May we take seriously his teaching
while welcoming those whose marriages
       have failed
and supporting them by our compassion and love.
Lord, hear us.

Priest/Leader

God of love,
you teach us that we must be like children
in welcoming your reign in our lives.
Help us to be open to your guiding Spirit
and to renew each day our hope in you.
We ask this through Christ our Lord. Amen.

SUNDAY 28   YEAR B

Priest/Leader

"For God all things are possible."
We are encouraged and strengthened
by the word of God;
and as followers of Jesus
we bring our needs to the Father.

1. For the gift of wisdom.
(pause)
May we be given the gift of wisdom
to help us achieve balance in our lives;
and may we value what is of lasting importance,
giving us insight into God's purposes
for ourselves and for our world.
Lord, hear us.

2. For a respect for God's word.
(pause)
God's word is alive and active,
probing to the depths of our being.
May we learn to respect God's word,
welcoming its teaching
to judge what we proclaim and how we live.
Lord, hear us.

3. For a right attitude toward wealth.
(pause)
May we be guided by gospel teaching
in our attitude toward wealth,
tempering our need for money and security
with a desire to be generous

as God commands.
Lord, hear us.

4. For generosity in working for God's reign.
(pause)
Jesus commands us to be serious about
the gospel.
May we be generous with our time and
resources
in working to establish God's rule in our world,
and may we be constant in our witness
to God's truth and justice and love.
Lord, hear us.

Priest/Leader

God of love,
you are the giver of all good things.
Fill us with confidence in you
that we may be faithful witnesses of the gospel.
We ask this through Christ our Lord. Amen.

SUNDAY 29   YEAR B

Priest/Leader

The Letter to the Hebrews encourages us to be
confident
in approaching the throne of grace.
We turn to our God, then,
asking what we need
for ourselves, our families, our church, and our
world.

1. For a right understanding of suffering.
(pause)
The innocent servant of God in Isaiah
suffered for the faults of many.
May we struggle to understand suffering in
our world
as part of the mysterious purposes of God
calling us to generosity of spirit toward those
in need.
Lord, hear us.

2. For renewed confidence in God.
(pause)
Jesus is our High Priest, the Son of God.
With him as our guide and brother,

may we be renewed in confidence
approaching the throne of grace
especially in times of trouble and suffering.
Lord, hear us.

3. For perseverance in witnessing to the gospel.
(pause)
May we persevere as disciples of Jesus,
living according to his teaching
and proclaiming gospel values
even when this leads
to rejection and condemnation.
Lord, hear us.

4. For a desire to be of service.
(pause)
May we follow the example of Jesus,
who came not to be served but to serve.
May we always be alert to the needs
of others,
not unwillingly
but generous in our service.
Lord, hear us.

Priest/Leader

God of all compassion,
teach us to be good followers of your Son,
who gave his life as a ransom for all.
We ask this through Christ our Lord. Amen.

SUNDAY 30   YEAR B

Priest/Leader

"Take heart; get up, he is calling you."
Strengthened by God's word broken for us,
we come in confidence to the Lord
with our needs and those of our world.

1. For the gift of being comforters.
(pause)
Just as God comforted the people of Israel,
gathering those whom the world rejected,
so may we be comforters especially of the weak.
May we be rich in hospitality, warm in our
welcoming,
and strong in our support of one another.
Lord, hear us.

2. For confidence in God's goodness and love.
(pause)
Christ is our High Priest
called from among us
to plead for us with the Father.
May his presence with God
renew our confidence in prayer to
    our God.
Lord, hear us.

3. For those who are seeking the truth.
(pause)
May those who are looking for truth
experience the healing touch of the Lord
and, being filled with courage,
acknowledge Jesus as the Messiah of God
and follow him on his way.
Lord, hear us.

4. For courage in following the Lord.
(pause)
May we be courageous in following the Lord,
obedient to the teaching of the gospel
through lives that bring healing and
    wholeness
to those in the community
who need our care.
Lord, hear us.

Priest/Leader

God of light,
help us see more clearly
the way you have planned for us.
Give us courage and perseverance
to follow you in our lives.
We ask this through Christ our Lord.
    Amen.

SUNDAY 31   YEAR B

Priest/Leader

"You are not far from the kingdom of God."
We have listened to God's word
and professed our faith.
Now with confidence we turn to God
for all our needs.

1. For a commitment to keep God's
    commandments.
(pause)
We are commanded to love God
all the days of our lives.
May we be constant in keeping God's
    commandments
and may the desire to serve God
be written in our hearts.
Lord, hear us.

2. For confidence in Christ, the High Priest.
(pause)
Christ is our High Priest
whose power to save is certain.
May we be comforted by his powerful presence
    with God
for he has been made the perfect one
who intercedes on our behalf forever.
Lord, hear us.

3. For a desire to love our neighbor as ourselves.
(pause)
Jesus teaches that the greatest commandment
is to love God by loving our neighbor.
May we grow in love of one another,
learning to forgive and to accept;
and may we become together the people that
    God wants.
Lord, hear us.

4. For a longing for the reign of God.
(pause)
May we be filled with a great desire
for the coming of God's reign.
May our struggle for justice and peace
and our concern for truth
witness our longing that God's will be done.
Lord, hear us.

Priest/Leader

God of love,
fill us with your blessings
so that we will be strong
in keeping your commandments
and constant in loving one another.
We ask this through Christ our Lord. Amen.

Priest/Leader

"Christ…entered into heaven itself,
now to appear in the presence of God on our
    behalf."
God's word is broken for us
and we have made our act of faith.
Now, with trust, we turn to our God,
recalling our needs.

1. For the gift of hospitality.
(pause)
Like the woman who welcomed Elijah,
and fed him from the little she had,
may we be a people of hospitality,
welcoming strangers into our community
with warmth and acceptance.
Lord, hear us.

2. For trust in God's merciful love.
(pause)
The Letter to the Hebrews
teaches that all will be judged.
Trusting in God's merciful love,
may we be comforted that Christ took on
    our faults
and promises salvation to those who wait for him.
Lord, hear us.

3. For the gift of sincerity.
(pause)
Jesus condemned the hypocrisy of his enemies.
May we too avoid hypocrisy
in our dealing with one another
and treat all people
with sincerity and honesty.
Lord, hear us.

4. For a spirit of generosity.
(pause)
Like the poor widow in the gospel story,
may we be generous in giving to the Lord,
learning to trust in God's goodness
so that we may be content with what we have
and generous toward others in need.
Lord, hear us.

Priest/Leader

God of love,
you sent your Son to be our Savior and our teacher.
Open our minds to his voice
and our hearts to follow his example.
We ask this through Christ our Lord. Amen.

SUNDAY 33   YEAR B

Priest/Leader

"Heaven and earth will pass away,
but my words will not pass away."
We have listened to the Bible readings,
God's word proclaimed for our nourishment.
Now we turn to God with confidence
for our needs and those of the church and
    the world.

1. For the gift of wisdom.
(pause)
May we acknowledge the mysterious purposes
    of God,
who alone knows the fate of our world;
and may we seek to be wise in the ways of God,
living by the commandments
to live with God for all eternity.
Lord, hear us.

2. For an understanding of what Christ has
    won for us.
(pause)
May we grow in understanding the mission of Jesus,
who offered himself to destroy sin
and is now with God forever;
and by lives that are faithful to his teaching
may we seek the perfection that God desires.
Lord, hear us.

3. For confidence in times of trial.
(pause)
May we acknowledge that God alone
is Lord of the universe
and that all things are in God's hands.
And may we be filled with confidence and trust
as we wait for the coming of the Lord.
Lord, hear us.

4. For joy in doing God's will.
(pause)
The teaching of Jesus lasts forever.
Even in times of confusion and unrest,
may we find joy and peace
in knowing that we are doing God's will
by our obedience to the gospel and the way of
    Christ.
Lord, hear us.

Priest/Leader

Eternal God,
our first beginning and our last end,
fill us with hope and confidence
and trust in your goodness.
We ask this through Christ our Lord. Amen.

FEAST OF CHRIST THE KING YEAR B

Priest/Leader

"For this I came into the world,
to testify to the truth."
We have listened to God's word
and now turn to God with confidence
for all our needs.

1. For an acceptance of God's providence.
(pause)
Sovereignty has been promised to God's holy one,
whom we proclaim as the Christ of God.
May we be consoled by God's providence,
living as God's servants
in a reign that lasts forever.
Lord, hear us.

2. For the gift of service.
(pause)
Christ is the firstborn of the dead,
the One who was and is and is to come.
May we witness to our faith in his glory
by lives of service
in the church and in the community.
Lord, hear us.

3. For an acceptance of Jesus our King.
(pause)
Jesus' kingdom is not of this world.

May we be true subjects of Jesus our King,
avoiding violence, promoting gentleness,
working for justice, seeking reconciliation,
and living by the light of the gospel.
Lord, hear us.

4. For a desire to witness to the truth.
(pause)
May we follow the example of Jesus our King,
listening to his teaching in every generation;
and may we be known as people of the truth,
bearing witness to the message of the gospel
in what we profess and how we live.
Lord, hear us.

Priest/Leader

Lord of the universe,
your Son Jesus established a kingdom
of justice, love, and peace.
Help us to live according to his teaching,
for he is Lord, forever and ever. Amen.

SUNDAY 2   YEAR C

Priest/Leader

"Jesus…revealed his glory;
and his disciples believed in him."
God's powerful word has been broken for us
and we have been nourished by its teaching.
Its message fills us with joy
as we turn to the Lord in prayer.

1. For a sense of joy in God's presence.
(pause)
May we be filled with joy
in the presence of the Lord,
knowing that our God
who takes delight in us
will not forsake us in times of trouble.
Lord, hear us.

2. For an appreciation of the gifts God gives us.
(pause)
The Spirit distributes different gifts
to different people.
May we be open to the gifts God gives,
eager to use them

for the service of others.
Lord, hear us.

3. For an awareness of God's abundant love.
(pause)
The water made into wine
is a sign of God's extravagant love.
May we always acknowledge the abundance of
     God's love
and show it forth
in lives of integrity and faithful witness.
Lord, hear us.

4. For a desire to listen to Jesus.
(pause)
Mary told the waiters
to do what Jesus told them.
May we be attentive to his teaching,
determined to follow his way
and to witness to his glory.
Lord, hear us.

Priest/Leader

God of abundant love,
we rejoice always in your love.
Hear the prayers we make
through Christ our Lord. Amen.

SUNDAY 3   YEAR C

Priest/Leader

"The Spirit of the Lord…has anointed me
to bring good news to the poor."
God's good news has been proclaimed for us.
Renewed and strengthened by that word,
we turn to our living God
for our needs and those of all the world.

1. For a renewed desire to do what God wants.
(pause)
The people of Israel rejoiced
when they discovered God's law that had
     been lost.
May we too rejoice in God's commandments,
eager to do what is right
as God's people in God's world.
Lord, hear us.

2. For a sense of belonging to the Lord.
(pause)
May we accept with humility
that each of us is important in the body
     of Christ.
May we affirm one another's gifts
and encourage our sisters and brothers
in the service of the community.
Lord, hear us.

3. For a deeper trust in God's promises.
(pause)
Jesus was filled with the Spirit of God
and proclaimed the fulfillment of God's
     promises.
May we who have been given the same Spirit
accept that we too are called
for the saving purposes of God.
Lord, hear us.

4. For the gift of living the gospel.
(pause)
Jesus was sent to bring good news to the poor.
May we too bring good news to people
by our faithfulness to gospel values,
proclaiming the Lord's year of favor
by our practice of the way of Christ.
Lord, hear us.

Priest/Leader

Creator God,
your Son brings life to the world.
Listen to the prayers of his faithful people
for we make them through the same Christ our
     Lord. Amen.

SUNDAY 4   YEAR C

Priest/Leader

"No prophet is accepted in the prophet's
     hometown."
We have listened to prophecy
and we have been nourished by the word of
     the Lord.
With confidence we turn to the Lord
for our needs and those of all the world.

1. For courage to be faithful to God's word.
(pause)
God formed us in our mother's womb;
God knew us there and owned us there.
May we have the courage and the confidence
to acknowledge God in our lives
and to be faithful to God's ways.
Lord, hear us.

2. For the gift of love.
(pause)
May we always be grateful for God's gift
    of love—
the greatest gift we have received;
and by our patience, kindness,
and concern for others,
may we live out that gift in all that we do.
Lord, hear us.

3. For prophets in the church.
(pause)
May we learn to respect prophets in
    our church
who read the signs of the times
in the light of God's word
and who teach us what God wants
in the church and in the community.
Lord, hear us.

4. For an acceptance of God's choices.
(pause)
God's ways and God's choices are not
    like ours.
May we be open to God's purposes,
alert to the unexpected voices
who recall to us
our responsibilities before our God.
Lord, hear us.

Priest/Leader

God of the universe,
you call us to faithful service
in the world and in the church.
Teach us the primacy of love
in all that we value; in all that we do.
We ask this through Christ our Lord.
        Amen.

Priest/Leader

"Here I am; send me!"
God's word tells us of faithful witnesses
and we in turn are called to lives of service.
Strengthened by that word,
we turn to our God for what we need.

1. For the gift of generosity in responding to God.
(pause)
May we be like Isaiah the prophet,
strong in faith and hope,
and eager to respond to God's call.
May we be conscious of God's forgiveness
and generous in our lives of service.
Lord, hear us.

2. For perseverance in doing God's will.
(pause)
May we be strong and patient in doing
    God's will,
and, like Paul, the least of the apostles,
may we cling to what we have been taught—
the good news about Jesus
and the generous love of our God.
Lord, hear us.

3. For those who spread the gospel.
(pause)
May those who are called to preach the
    good news
be encouraged to break that word
with integrity and compassion
so that the gospel of the Lord
may be made known throughout the world.
Lord, hear us.

4. For the gift of courage.
(pause)
Jesus commands us not to be afraid of
    our weakness
but to have confidence in God's power to save.
May we have courage to persevere
in living out the gospel
by lives of service and concern for others.
Lord, hear us.

Priest/Leader

God of consolation,
you call us to service
in the church and in the world.
Grant us what we need
to be faithful followers of your Son,
who is Lord, forever and ever. Amen.

SUNDAY 6   YEAR C

Priest/Leader

"Rejoice…and leap for joy,
for surely your reward is great in heaven."
The good news of Jesus Christ
fills us with joy;
and as children of our living God
we turn to the Lord in prayer.

1. For trust in God.
(pause)
God's word declares blessed
those who trust in the Lord.
May we be people who trust in God,
bearing fruit for God
by lives of integrity.
Lord, hear us.

2. For renewed faith in the risen Christ.
(pause)
Christ has been raised from the dead,
the first fruit of those who have fallen asleep.
May we be renewed in our faith in the
     risen Christ
and live as people of hope,
trusting in God's promise of eternal life.
Lord, hear us.

3. For a deep commitment to the way
     of Jesus.
(pause)
The Beatitudes of Jesus
teach us what is of value in life.
May we be more and more convinced
of his teaching
and committed to live by his way.
Lord, hear us.

4. For a desire to live as God commands.
(pause)
May we be moved by the teaching of Jesus
to live as his disciples in the world,
professing our faith in God's purposes
by following the Beatitudes of Jesus
in all that we do.
Lord, hear us.

Priest/Leader

God of all ages,
we renew our trust in you.
Grant what we need
in our community and in our world.
We ask this through Christ our Lord. Amen.

SUNDAY 7   YEAR C

Priest/Leader

"Be merciful, just as your Father is merciful."
God's word disturbs us—
it turns our values upside down.
Yet with faith in our God who saves us,
we turn in prayer for what we need.

1. For the gift of compassion.
(pause)
David spared the life of Saul,
the anointed one of God.
May we too be people of compassion,
aware of the dignity of others
with whom we live in the community.
Lord, hear us.

2. For a desire to be like Christ.
(pause)
May we model ourselves on God's risen Son,
who humbled himself
to share our human condition.
May we strive to be like him
in how we live and what we value.
Lord, hear us.

3. For the grace of forgiveness.
(pause)
May we forgive others as God forgives us,
returning blessing for curses

from those who hate us.
And may we never be resentful
but strive to live as children of our God.
Lord, hear us.

4. For a spirit of gentleness.
(pause)
Jesus commands us to be generous—
with time, with money, with affection.
May we be people of love,
accepting and pardoning one another
in the name of God.
Lord, hear us.

Priest/Leader

God of compassion,
teach us your ways
and help us to live
as sisters and brothers of your Son,
who is Lord, forever and ever. Amen.

SUNDAY 8   YEAR C

Priest/Leader

"No good tree bears bad fruit."
God's word has been broken for us
and has nourished us.
We now turn to our loving God
for our needs and those of all the world.

1. For care in what we say.
(pause)
Scripture commands us to speak the truth.
May we be aware of the power of speech
to hurt and destroy;
and may we seek always to temper our judgments
with compassion and justice.
Lord, hear us.

2. For renewed trust in God's promises.
(pause)
Paul teaches that, since Christ is risen,
death no longer has any power over us.
May we be comforted by this teaching,
believing the promises of victory
through God's own Son.
Lord, hear us.

3. For integrity in our lives.
(pause)
May we be constant
in what we value in life;
and may we so live by the teaching of the gospel
that we may be fruitful for God
through the integrity of our lives.
Lord, hear us.

4. For a right attitude toward what is of value.
(pause)
May we avoid hypocrisy in our lives,
proclaiming to live by one standard
yet living by others;
and may we be concerned for gospel values
as faithful disciples of Jesus our teacher.
Lord, hear us.

Priest/Leader

God of mercy,
be compassionate toward us
in your kindness;
and grant what we need
through Christ our Lord. Amen.

SUNDAY 9   YEAR C

Priest/Leader

"Not even in Israel
have I found such faith."
God's word helps us understand God's purposes.
Strengthened by its message,
we ask our God for what we need.

1. For an acceptance of people everywhere.
(pause)
The Bible teaches that God has no favorites
but loves and accepts all people.
May we be open to other people
and welcome strangers into our community
as God commands.
Lord, hear us.

2. For faithfulness in following the good news.
(pause)
Paul commands us to be faithful
in following the good news we have heard.

May we try always to live by the gospel,
searching for what is of value in God's sight
as servants of the Christ.
Lord, hear us.

3. For an awareness of God's goodness in others.
(*pause*)
May we be tolerant and welcoming of other people
—especially those of different cultures and traditions—
aware that God's choices are not our choices
and that God's gift of faith
is not limited by any human tradition.
Lord, hear us.

4. For faith in God's power to heal.
(*pause*)
Like the centurion in the gospel,
may we confess God's power to heal,
acknowledging the authority of God's word
that restores to health
all who call on God's name.
Lord, hear us.

Priest/Leader

All powerful God,
you show your love for all people in the world.
Grant what we need to be your faithful people.
We ask this through Christ our Lord. Amen.

SUNDAY 10   YEAR C

Priest/Leader

"'A great prophet has risen among us!'
and 'God has looked favorably on his people!'"
God's word strengthens us on life's journey.
With renewed faith in God's power to save,
we turn to our God for what we need.

1. For an awareness of God's gift of life.
(*pause*)
Through Elijah's faith and prayer,
the child was restored to life.
May we acknowledge
that all life is God's gift
to be lived as God commands.
Lord, hear us.

2. For a desire to be faithful to the gospel.
(*pause*)
Paul struggled to know what God
wanted of him.
May we too acknowledge the cost of
faithfulness,
striving to be faithful to the good news
and witnessing to its power
in the church and in the community.
Lord, hear us.

3. For those who are bereaved.
(*pause*)
Jesus raised the son of the widow of Nain.
May we be his good followers,
comforting those who are in mourning
and consoling them by our prayers and concern
in their time of loss.
Lord, hear us.

4. For prophets in the church and in the
community.
(*pause*)
In Christ, God has visited the people.
May we respect those in the church and
the community
who call us to live according to the gospel,
reminding us of God's power to save
and to bring us all to life forever.
Lord, hear us.

Priest/Leader

God of the living and the dead,
you are the source of all life.
Grant what we need,
especially in time of sorrow.
We ask this through Christ our Lord. Amen.

SUNDAY 11   YEAR C

Priest/Leader

"It is no longer I who live,
but it is Christ who lives in me."
God's good news astonishes us with its message
and comforts us with its boldness.
Strengthened by its teaching,
we ask our God for what we need.

1. For a desire to live as God wants.
(pause)
God's forgiveness is lavish
when we turn from our sins.
May we follow the example of David,
who repented of his wrongdoing
and received the gift of life.
Lord, hear us.

2. For a deeper understanding of Christ's
    love for us.
(pause)
With Christ we have been crucified
and his risen life is ours in baptism.
May we live according to his teaching,
believing the good news
that brings wholeness to our lives.
Lord, hear us.

3. For a desire to show forth love in action.
(pause)
May our desire to live as God wants
make us eager to care for one another
in the church and in the community;
and may we learn from our Teacher
to wash one another's feet in love and service.
Lord, hear us.

4. For a spirit of generosity.
(pause)
May we imitate the women who followed Jesus,
generous in his service
and faithful in their witness;
and may we follow the example of the Lord,
refusing to condemn those whom
        society rejects.
Lord, hear us.

Priest/Leader

God of the promise,
may your kingdom come!
Forgive us when we fail;
encourage us in faith.
We ask this through Christ our Lord.
        Amen.

Priest/Leader

"Those who lose their life for my sake will save it."
God's good news challenges us to consider
what is important in life.
Nourished by that teaching,
we turn to our God for what we need.

1. For a spirit of kindness and prayer.
(pause)
God's gift to the people of Jerusalem
was a spirit of kindness and prayer.
May that spirit be ours too,
a sign of God's consolation
in times of sorrow and loss.
Lord, hear us.

2. For unity in the church and in the community.
 (pause)
Through baptism, we have become
        God's children,
clothed in Christ, without distinction.
May we be conscious of our unity
in the church and in the community,
united in our desire to live as God wants.
Lord, hear us.

3. For the gift of faith.
(pause)
Peter confessed Jesus as the Christ of God.
May we grow in faith about Jesus,
accepting him as God's chosen one
in the tradition of the prophets
who teach us the ways of God.
Lord, hear us.

4. For the strength to carry our cross.
(pause)
May we be constant in following our Master,
even at the cost of rejection;
and may we who are his disciples
carry one another's crosses
as together we follow the way of the Lord.
Lord, hear us.

Priest/Leader

God of all consolation,
you are the giver of all good things.
Listen to the prayers we make
through Christ our Lord. Amen.

SUNDAY 13   YEAR C

Priest/Leader

"No one who puts a hand to the plow and looks back
is fit for the kingdom of God."
The words of Jesus remind us of the cost
of being disciples.
Yet strengthened by God's word
and resolved to be good disciples,
we bring our needs before our God.

1. For a deep resolve to be faithful followers.
(pause)
Elisha destroyed his yoke and oxen
to show his resolve to be a disciple.
May we too be strong in our commitment
to be faithful followers of the Lord
by lives of honesty, justice, and truth.
Lord, hear us.

2. For service in the community.
(pause)
We are free from the slavery of sin
and called to lives of service.
May we be guided by God's Spirit
to avoid selfishness in our lives
and to give ourselves in love for others.
Lord, hear us.

3. For a desire to spread the gospel.
(pause)
May we be moved by Jesus' command
to spread the good news,
and by lives that reflect gospel teaching
show forth the way of Christ
in all we value, in all we profess.
Lord, hear us.

4. For the community that is called the church.
(pause)
May the church everywhere

take seriously the call to discipleship;
and may all of us
who bear the name of Christian
be faithful in our witness to the gospel.
Lord, hear us.

Priest/Leader

Lord God of our ancestors,
your Son is the way, the truth, and the life.
Help us in our resolve to follow him,
for he is Lord, forever and ever. Amen.

SUNDAY 14   YEAR C

Priest/Leader

"Rejoice that your names are written in heaven."
God's word consoles us and comforts us,
and its teaching is food for our journey.
We turn, then, to our God
for all we need in the church and in the community.

1. For the gift of peace.
(pause)
Peace was God's gift to the people of old
and, in every generation, God renews that gift,
like a mother nourishing her child.
May we rejoice in God's gift of peace
and may it console us in times of trouble.
Lord, hear us.

2. For an acceptance of the mystery of the cross.
(pause)
Paul boasted about the cross of Jesus,
accepting its mystery for his journey in faith.
May we too be open to God's purposes,
professing the mystery of God's love
by our love and acceptance of one another.
Lord, hear us.

3. For a right attitude toward possessions.
(pause)
Jesus commanded his followers
to live lives of simplicity and trust.
May we have a right attitude to what we possess
and may we be generous in sharing what we have
for the sake of God's reign.
Lord, hear us.

4. For trust in God.
(pause)
In times of persecution and hardship,
may we know that God is near;
and may we be comforted by God's promises
that those who live by the gospel
have their names written in heaven.
Lord, hear us.

Priest/Leader

God of all consolation,
you are faithful to your promises.
Help us to be faithful followers of your Son,
who is Lord, forever and ever. Amen.

SUNDAY 15   YEAR C

Priest/Leader

"Go and do likewise."
We have listened to God's word
and been nourished by its teaching.
We now recall what we need
in the church and in the community.

1. For a desire to keep God's commandments.
(pause)
We are called to obey God's laws,
revealed in the Bible and in our hearts.
May we be constant in discerning God's will
for how we are to live
in the church and in the community.
Lord, hear us.

2. For a deep devotion to Christ.
(pause)
Christ is the head of the church,
the firstborn of the dead.
May we deepen our devotion to Christ,
the image of the unseen God,
who has established peace by his death on the cross.
Lord, hear us.

3. For those in need in society.
(pause)
Jesus teaches us to have pity
on one another.
Like the Good Samaritan,

may we be generous toward those in society
who are suffering and in need.
Lord, hear us.

4. For the grace to love one another.
(pause)
The greatest of the commandments
is to love God and one another.
May we be constant in living out that command,
avoiding what is hurtful to others
in what we say and what we do.
Lord, hear us.

Priest/Leader

God of all kindness,
you reveal your love for us in the death of your Son.
Help us to be generous in our love for others.
We ask this through Christ our Lord. Amen.

SUNDAY 16   YEAR C

Priest/Leader

"There is need of only one thing."
The good news urges us to consider
our priorities in life.
Strengthened by God's word,
we approach our God
for what we need.

1. For the gift of hospitality.
(pause)
Abraham welcomed the strangers into
    his community
and was rewarded for his generosity.
May we too be a community that is open
    to others,
welcoming strangers in the name of our God
and inviting them to be at home among us.
Lord, hear us.

2. For faithfulness in proclaiming the teaching of
    Jesus.
(pause)
May the community that is called the church
be faithful in every generation
in proclaiming God's mysterious purposes.
May we be faithful witnesses of the Christ

who is our hope of glory.
Lord, hear us.

3. For what is important in life.
(*pause*)
Jesus teaches us to reflect on God's word,
and to spend time in considering
what God reveals as important in life.
May we be guided by the teaching of
        the gospel
in deciding what is of lasting value for us.
Lord, hear us.

4. For the gift of really listening.
(*pause*)
May we learn to listen to one another
in the church and in the community;
may we not be distracted
from what matters most
in following the Christ.
Lord, hear us.

Priest/Leader

God of all goodness,
you are generous to your people
in what we have and in what you
        promise.
Listen to the prayers we offer
through Christ our Lord. Amen.

SUNDAY 17   YEAR C

Priest/Leader

"Lord, teach us to pray."
We have listened to God's word
and been nourished by its teaching.
Now we reflect on what we need
and present our needs before our God.

1. For perseverance in prayer.
(*pause*)
By his perseverance in prayer,
Abraham pleaded with God
to spare the people of Sodom.
May we too be persistent in our prayer
as we seek to be faithful to the Lord.
Lord, hear us.

2. For a sense of new life in Christ.
(*pause*)
We have been buried with Christ
and raised to new life in him.
May we rejoice in our unity with Christ,
acknowledging the forgiveness of all sin
for those who share his life with God.
Lord, hear us.

3. For a right attitude to prayer.
(*pause*)
May we always acknowledge our God
as creator and ruler of all;
and may our prayers reflect our faith
in God's goodness and in our acceptance
of the mystery of God's purposes.
Lord, hear us.

4. For an appreciation of God's generous love.
(*pause*)
The gospel teaches us about God's generous love
and the Spirit of God that is given to us.
May this teaching help us to pray—
to ask, to search, and to look for doors
that God opens for us in life.
Lord, hear us.

Priest/Leader

God of surprises,
you give your Spirit to those who ask.
Fill us with your gifts
and grant what we need
through Christ our Lord. Amen.

SUNDAY 18   YEAR C

Priest/Leader

"Christ is all and in all!"
God's word has been broken for us
and its teaching is food for our journey.
We now turn to our God
for what we need
in the church and in the community.

1. For a right attitude to what we possess.
(*pause*)
The word of God commands us to be careful

about what is important in life.
May we learn to obey that teaching
and to have a right attitude
about what is of lasting value.
Lord, hear us.

2. For a desire to live as God wants.
(pause)
In baptism, we put on Christ
and resolved to follow the way of the Lord.
May our oneness in Christ
lead us to accept one another
as God commands.
Lord, hear us.

3. For a desire to be rich in God's sight.
(pause)
When we are persuaded that possessions alone
will bring happiness and fulfillment,
may we be moved by the teaching of Jesus
to be careful about the desire for riches,
except the desire to be rich in God's sight.
Lord, hear us.

4. For an appreciation of what makes us secure
      in life.
(pause)
Jesus teaches us to be on our guard
against greed of any kind.
May we search for real security in life
by seeking to do God's will
and by lives that reflect gospel values.
Lord, hear us.

Priest/Leader

God of all goodness,
you are generous in what you give us.
Help us to know what is of lasting value in life.
We ask this through Christ our Lord. Amen.

SUNDAY 19   YEAR C

Priest/Leader

"Where your treasure is, there will your heart be
      also."
God's word has been broken for us,
giving us strength for life's journey.

We now turn to our God for what we need
in the church and in the community.

1. For courage to be faithful.
(pause)
We are commanded to have courage
in following the will of our God,
confessing that we belong to the
      chosen people
who from ancient times
have struggled to do God's will.
Lord, hear us.

2. For a greater faith in the God of the promises.
(pause)
Our ancestor Abraham is a model of faith
for us and for all who follow the Lord.
May his courage and his obedience to what
      God wanted
inspire us to be faithful in our own time
in discerning God's will for how we are to live.
Lord, hear us.

3. For trust in God.
(pause)
Jesus tells us there is no need
to be afraid,
for we belong to God's people.
May this teaching comfort us in times
      of trouble
and encourage us to place our trust in our God.
Lord, hear us.

4. For the need to be ready for God.
(pause)
God comes into our lives
at unexpected times and in unexpected ways.
May we be alert to the signs of the times,
ready to respond to God's purposes
in the church and in the community.
Lord, hear us.

Priest/Leader

God of the promises,
you are constant in caring for your people.
Grant what we need to be faithful.
We ask this through Christ our Lord.
      Amen.

Priest/Leader

"I have come to bring fire to the earth."
God's word is sharper than a two-edged sword,
demanding action from us and not words only.
Strengthened by God's word,
we turn to the Lord for what we need.

1. For courage to be witnesses to the truth.
(*pause*)
Jeremiah was persecuted for what
        he believed
but remained faithful to God's commands.
May we too not lose heart
but be given the courage
to be faithful to what God wants.
Lord, hear us.

2. For perseverance in faith.
(*pause*)
We are encouraged in our life of faith
by the great cloud of witnesses
in the church and in the world.
May we never lose sight of Jesus,
our leader in faith, who is at God's right hand.
Lord, hear us.

3. For a sense of urgency in doing God's will.
(*pause*)
Jesus longed and longed for the coming of
        God's reign.
May we too be convinced
about the demands that the gospel makes
        upon us;
and, by lives that reflect the teaching of Jesus,
bring the fire of God's love upon the earth.
Lord, hear us.

4. For understanding the radical demands
        of the gospel.
(*pause*)
Jesus promises conflict
to those who take the gospel seriously.
May our following the way of Christ
be central to our lives
even at the cost of suffering.
Lord, hear us.

Priest/Leader

God of all ages,
may your kingdom come!
Comfort us in difficult times
and grant what we ask
through Christ our Lord. Amen.

SUNDAY 21   YEAR C

Priest/Leader

"Some are last who will be first,
and some are first who will be last."
The paradoxes of God's word
disturb and challenge us.
We have listened to that word
and now turn to God for what we need.

1. For an understanding of God's love for all people.
(*pause*)
The Lord will gather the nations of every language.
May we grow in understanding
that God's love is for all people;
and may we strive to be faithful in our witness
to the glory of our God.
Lord, hear us.

2. For a deep sense of being God's children.
(*pause*)
May we be comforted by the teaching
that we are indeed the children of God,
and even in times of suffering and loss
proclaim God's love
for all God's people.
Lord, hear us.

3. For a desire to take the gospel seriously.
(*pause*)
May we be moved by the demands of the gospel,
not taking it lightly
but striving to make it part of our lives,
knowing that this is what God commands
to those who look for promised salvation.
Lord, hear us.

4. For an awareness that God's ways are not our ways.
(*pause*)
Jesus teaches us

that the first will be last and the last first.
May we acknowledge that God's ways are not
    our ways,
and that only God knows what is in our hearts
and how we are valued in God's sight.
Lord, hear us.

Priest/Leader

God of the promises,
you call us to be perfect
in following the way of Jesus.
Listen to the prayers we make.
We ask this through Christ our Lord. Amen.

SUNDAY 22   YEAR C

Priest/Leader

"All who exalt themselves will be humbled,
and those who humble themselves will be exalted."
God's word nourishes us and challenges us.
That word has been broken for us
and with confidence
we turn to our God for what we need.

1. For a spirit of gentleness.
(pause)
God commands us to be gentle
in our dealings with one another.
May we be sensitive to the needs of others,
responding to them with kindness
and finding favor with the Lord.
Lord, hear us.

2. For a deeper understanding of God's love for us.
(pause)
We are the people of the new covenant
and we confess Jesus as our mediator with God.
May we be renewed in our confidence
in the One who calls us to perfection
in the city of the living God.
Lord, hear us.

3. For the gift of humility.
(pause)
Jesus commands us to be careful about false values
and self-importance in our dealing with others.
May we be aware of our worth as God's children,

not seeking power and status for ourselves
but eager, like our Master, to be of service to others.
Lord, hear us.

4. For the gift of generous love.
(pause)
Jesus teaches us to be generous
especially to those who have nothing to give in
    return.
May we be moved to kindness and charity in
    all things,
following the example of Jesus,
who gave his life for all.
Lord, hear us.

Priest/Leader

God of love, your concern for us
exceeds all that we look for.
Help us to be generous
in our dealings with others.
We ask this through Christ our Lord. Amen.

SUNDAY 23   YEAR C

Priest/Leader

"None of you can become my disciple
if you do not give up all your possessions."
We have reflected on God's word
proclaimed and broken for us.
Strengthened by its teaching
we turn to the Lord for what we need.

1. For a desire to know our God.
(pause)
In our search to understand the purposes of God,
may we be guided by the Holy Spirit—
God's Wisdom who teaches us all things:
about God and about ourselves
and about how we are to live as God wants.
Lord, hear us.

2. For a desire to be generous in God's sight.
(pause)
Paul asks us to be forgiving,
generous, and accepting of one another.
May we grow in love for each other,
confessing that what binds us together

is the blood of Christ.
Lord, hear us.

3. For a greater understanding about being a disciple.
(*pause*)
Jesus' teaching about being a disciple
disturbs and challenges us.
May we learn to carry one another's crosses
so that together we may be faithful
in following his way.
Lord, hear us.

4. For a deeper commitment to Christ.
(*pause*)
Jesus commands us to take seriously
the call to be a disciple.
May we be faithful in witnessing
to the truth about God
and the teaching of the gospel.
Lord, hear us.

Priest/Leader

God of all love,
you call us to faithful service
in the community and in the church.
Help us to be good servants of your Son,
for he is Lord, forever and ever. Amen.

SUNDAY 24   YEAR C

Priest/Leader

"This brother of yours was dead and has come to life;
he was lost and has been found."
God's word is food for our journey through life.
Its teaching strengthens us
and encourages us on the way.
In a spirit of thankfulness, we recall our needs before
    our God.

1. For the gift of forgiveness.
(*pause*)
Moses pleaded for the people of Israel
and God forgave their blasphemy.
May we also be generous in forgiving one another,
looking for ways to heal injuries
and restore friendships.
Lord, hear us.

2. For an openness to God's mercy.
(*pause*)
Christ Jesus came to save sinners.
May we be open to receive God's healing love
so that we might have life in its fullness
and experience the wholeness
that comes from following the way of Christ.
Lord, hear us.

3. For an appreciation of God's extravagant love.
(*pause*)
The gospel stories tell of the lengths
to which God goes to show love and acceptance.
May we be moved by these stories
to appreciate God's love for each of us
and to respond by lives of forgiveness and love.
Lord, hear us.

4. For a desire to accept others in the community.
(*pause*)
May we be generous in our acceptance of others,
slow to judge, quick to forgive;
and may God's abundant love for each of us
encourage us to care for one another
as shepherds care for their sheep.
Lord, hear us.

Priest/Leader

God of surprises,
you surround us with your love and forgiveness.
Teach us to be faithful to the gospel.
We ask this through Christ our Lord. Amen.

SUNDAY 25   YEAR C

Priest/Leader:

"You cannot serve God and wealth."
We have been nourished by God's word,
and its message both comforts and disturbs us.
We reflect on its meaning for our lives
and ask God for what we need.

1. For a strong sense of justice.
(*pause*)
The prophet Amos proclaims God's anger
against those who cheat the poor.
May we be honest in our dealings with one another

and always seek justice for those oppressed
in our society and in our world.
Lord, hear us.

2. For the need for prayer in our lives.
(*pause*)
Paul commands us to be people of prayer.
May we be true disciples of Jesus,
faithful in our lives of prayer,
witnessing to the gospel
and its meaning for our time.
Lord, hear us.

3. For single-mindedness in proclaiming
    gospel values.
(*pause*)
May we learn from the teaching of Jesus
to be single-minded in living by the gospel;
and by lives of integrity and truth
may we be witnesses to the Lord
by how we live and what we value.
Lord, hear us.

4. For a right attitude toward money.
(*pause*)
In our attitude toward money and possessions,
may we be guided by the teaching of
    the gospel.
May we be generous with what we have,
and trustworthy in our dealings with others
as children of the light.
Lord, hear us.

Priest/Leader

God of all consolation,
you are the giver of all good things.
Teach us to be content with what we have
and to be generous in your service.
We ask this through Christ our Lord.
    Amen.

SUNDAY 26   YEAR C

Priest/Leader

"Fight the good fight of the faith."
Strengthened by God's word,
proclaimed and broken for us,

we turn to our God
for courage to live its message
in the church and in society.

1. For a right attitude toward possessions.
(*pause*)
Amos preaches God's condemnation
of those who are in love with possessions.
May we be careful about what we value
and generous in sharing what we have
with those in need.
Lord, hear us.

2. For a desire to be witnesses to the truth.
(*pause*)
Like Timothy, we are called
to witness to the truth.
May we be constant in fighting the good fight
by saintly and religious lives
that reflect gospel values and the way
    of Christ.
Lord, hear us.

3. For a conviction about living as God wants.
(*pause*)
May we be conscious that we are God's people,
followers of the one who gave his life for all;
and may we be strong in our conviction
of the teaching of Jesus
about what is important in life.
Lord, hear us.

4. For a concern for the poor in society.
(*pause*)
May we be moved by the message of the gospel
to consider the poor in our society.
May our concern for their needs
be reflected in our generous use of time
    and money
and our promotion of justice in our world.
Lord, hear us.

Priest/Leader

God of all consolation,
you have a special love for the poor.
Teach us to have that love and concern,
and grant what we need.
We ask this through Christ our Lord. Amen.

SUNDAY 27   YEAR C

Priest/Leader

"Increase our faith!"
We have listened to God's word,
and its message is food for our journey
      through life.
Strengthened by its teaching,
we turn to our God for what we need.

1. For a desire to live by faith.
(pause)
God's message is to be patient
and to believe the promises that have been made.
May we acknowledge our God as Lord of the
      universe
and live by faith in God's power
to bring about God's purposes for us.
Lord, hear us.

2. For a desire to witness to the truth.
(pause)
May the Spirit of God be poured into
      our hearts;
and may we rely on God's power
to be strong in our desire
to witness to Jesus' teaching
by lives of love and self-control.
Lord, hear us.

3. For an openness to God's power in our lives.
(pause)
May we be open to the God of surprises
who commands us to be strong in faith.
May we be so renewed by God's Spirit
that the teaching and example of Jesus
may be evident in how we live each day.
Lord, hear us.

4. For an attitude of thanksgiving toward God.
(pause)
Faith is God's free gift to us,
given in love, strengthened in love.
May we be people who thank God always,
aware that we are God's servants
doing God's work in God's world.
Lord, hear us.

Priest/Leader

God of love,
fill us with your Spirit.
Comfort and encourage us
and increase the faith you have given us.
We ask this through Christ our Lord. Amen.

SUNDAY 28   YEAR C

Priest/Leader

"Your faith has made you well."
The word of God is food for our journey,
and we have been strengthened by its teaching.
Now we turn to our God
for what we need
in the church and in the community.

1. For an attitude of thankfulness toward God.
(pause)
Like Naaman the leper,
may we be thankful to God
for happiness and wholeness in our lives;
and like him may our thanks be measured
by lives of service in the name of our God.
Lord, hear us.

2. For thanksgiving for the good news.
(pause)
May we be constantly thankful
for the good news that cannot be chained.
May its message of hope and promise of life
comfort us and strengthen us
in time of hardship and trouble.
Lord, hear us.

3. For tolerance in our society.
(pause)
May we practice gospel values
in our relations to those on the margins of society,
and recall that those whom people rejected
were accepted and loved by Jesus,
who commands us to live his way.
Lord, hear us.

4. For a deeper faith in God's goodness.
(pause)
It is faith that saves us and makes us whole.

May we grow in faith each day
and, by our following of the way of Jesus,
show forth our faith
in lives of thankfulness, integrity, and love.
Lord, hear us.

Priest/Leader

God of all truth,
send your Spirit into our hearts
so that we may grow in love
as you command.
We ask this through Christ our Lord. Amen.

SUNDAY 29   YEAR C

Priest/Leader

"Will not God grant justice
to his chosen ones?"
The word of God cuts more sharply
than a double-edged sword.
Encouraged by its teaching,
we turn to our God for what we need.

1. For perseverance in prayer.
(*pause*)
Like Moses, may we be persistent in prayer,
searching to understand God's purposes
for us and for our world;
and may our prayers express our constant hope
for the coming of God's reign.
Lord, hear us.

2. For a love of the scriptures.
(*pause*)
Paul teaches us to love the scripture of God.
May it always be for us a source
of wisdom and good teaching;
and may its message
help us witness to the truth of God.
Lord, hear us.

3. For a desire for justice.
(*pause*)
May the teaching of Jesus move us
to a concern for justice, especially for the poor
and those whom society ignores;
and may we share Christ's longing

for justice in our world.
Lord, hear us.

4. For a deepening of our lives of prayer.
(*pause*)
May we relish the time we spend in prayer,
using those times for renewing and strengthening
        faith;
and may we never lose heart
but deepen our desire to be faithful followers
of the Son of man.
Lord, hear us.

Priest/Leader

Eternal God of heaven and earth,
we confess you as Lord of all.
Listen to the prayers we make
and grant what we need
through Christ our Lord. Amen.

SUNDAY 30   YEAR C

Priest/Leader

"All who exalt themselves will be humbled,
but all who humble themselves will be exalted."
God's word is good news
for our journey through life.
Strengthened by its teaching,
we ask our God for what we need.

1. For the gift of perseverance in prayer.
(*pause*)
The Lord listens to the prayers of the people.
May we grow in our life of prayer,
serving God with all our hearts
and open to God's purposes
for us and for our world.
Lord, hear us.

2. For courage to bear witness to Christ.
(*pause*)
Paul fought the good fight
and gave his life for the gospel of Jesus.
May we have courage to witness to the Lord
by lives that are faithful to the gospel
in our concern for justice and truth.
Lord, hear us.

3. For a sense of humility before the Lord.
(pause)
May we be filled with a sense of wonder
before our God,
open to God's promptings in the church
and in the community,
seeking always to live as God wants.
Lord, hear us.

4. For a desire to avoid pride.
(pause)
May we have a true sense
of our own worth before God,
not flaunting what God has given
but accepting ourselves and our gifts
with humility and thanksgiving.
Lord, hear us.

Priest/Leader

God of all ages,
may your kingdom come!
Teach us to have a right attitude
toward you and the people you love.
We ask this through Christ our Lord. Amen.

SUNDAY 31   YEAR C

Priest/Leader

"The Son of Man came to seek out
and to save the lost."
The word of God nourishes us with its message.
We now turn to our God for what we need
in the church and in the community.

1. For a deeper understanding of God's greatness.
(pause)
May we grow in understanding God's greatness,
aware that, for the Lord,
the world is like a grain of dust;
and may we be thankful for God's merciful love
and concern for us all.
Lord, hear us.

2. For a desire to be worthy of God's call.
(pause)
We have been called to be disciples of Jesus
and to live the gospel in our time.

May we be worthy of that calling
and, by the integrity of our lives,
give glory to our God.
Lord, hear us.

3. For an appreciation of the salvation offered
        by God.
(pause)
The salvation of God, achieved in Christ,
brings healing and wholeness to all people.
May we too be open to God's call
to seek out the lost and the lonely
and to accept others as God accepts us.
Lord, hear us.

4. For those whom society rejects.
(pause)
Zacchaeus was despised within his own community
but accepted and transformed by the love of Jesus.
May we be bearers of that same love,
bringing wholeness to all people,
especially those whom society rejects.
Lord, hear us.

Priest/Leader

God of our ancestors,
you have loved all people
since the beginning of time.
Fill us with your love and grant what we need
through Christ our Lord. Amen.

SUNDAY 32   YEAR C

Priest/Leader

"He is God not of the dead, but of the living;
for to him all of them are alive."
God's word has been proclaimed
and broken for us.
Nourished by its teaching,
we turn to our God in prayer
for our needs and those of the community.

1. For courage to witness to the truth.
(pause)
The Maccabees suffered for what they believed.
May we have courage to rely on God's promises,
witnessing to the truth we have received

about the purposes of God
by lives that are faithful to God's commandments.
Lord, hear us.

2. For thanksgiving for God's gifts.
(pause)
God has given us comfort and hope
to strengthen us as followers of Jesus.
May we be thankful for those gifts;
and may we be renewed
in our resolve to live by the gospel.
Lord, hear us.

3. For a sure hope in God's promises.
(pause)
The Bible is the story of God's faithfulness.
May its teaching and the faith we profess
convince us of the certainty of God's promises
about what is to come in this life
and in the next.
Lord, hear us.

4. For consolation in the face of death.
(pause)
May we be comforted by the teaching of the gospel
that those who have died
are alive to God;
and may we be strong in professing the risen Christ
who is Lord of the living and the dead.
Lord, hear us.

Priest/Leader

Eternal God, to you all people are alive.
Console us with your truth
and grant what we need
through Christ our Lord. Amen.

SUNDAY 33   YEAR C

Priest/Leader

"By your endurance you will gain your souls."
We have listened to God's word,
proclaimed and broken for us.
Now we turn to our God for what we need
in the church and in the community.

1. For righteousness before God.
(pause)
May we wait for the Lord in patience,
knowing that God's time is not
            our time.
And in the Day of the Lord,
may we be counted among those
who honor God's name.
Lord, hear us.

2. For the gift of discernment.
(pause)
Paul warns us against foolishness
in interpreting the coming of the Lord.
May we have the gift of discernment
to acknowledge the mysterious purposes
            of God
about what is planned for our world.
Lord, hear us.

3. For the gift of patience.
(pause)
May we be careful not to be deceived
by those who claim to come in Christ's name,
but, through our patience and perseverance
in living by the gospel,
bear witness that each day is the Day of
            the Lord.
Lord, hear us.

4. For the gift of endurance.
(pause)
Jesus warned of persecutions and stress.
May we be filled by God's Spirit
so that we will be strong in faith
and constant in hope,
witnessing to the teaching of Jesus.
Lord, hear us.

Priest/Leader

God of all ages,
may your kingdom come!
Help us to be faithful always
to the teaching of your Son.
We ask this through Christ our Lord.
        Amen.

FEAST OF CHRIST THE KING YEAR C

Priest/Leader

"Today you will be with me in Paradise."
The good news of Christ the King
brings us joy and consolation.
Strengthened by God's word,
we turn to the Lord for what we need.

1. For a desire to serve one another.
(*pause*)
David was chosen by God to be the shepherd
of the people of Israel.
May we be shepherds to one another
by the strength of our love
and the depth of our care.
Lord, hear us.

2. For an awareness of the majesty of Christ.
(*pause*)
All perfection is found in Christ,
who has made peace with God
through his death on the cross.
May we be comforted by the majesty of Christ
as Son of God and head of the church.
Lord, hear us.

3. For the gift of repentance.
(*pause*)
Like the good thief,
may we acknowledge wrongdoing,
conscious that the love of Christ
will overcome all fear and sin
and lead us to the promised paradise.
Lord, hear us.

4. For an understanding of the reign
    of Christ.
(*pause*)
May we be constant in living
as servants of Jesus;
and by the values we profess
help bring about God's reign in our world
and wholeness to all its people.
Lord, hear us.

Priest/Leader

God of love,
we honor Jesus as our ruler.
Help us to be his good servants
and faithful to his teaching.
We ask this through Christ our Lord.
    Amen.

FEAST DAYS

PRESENTATION OF THE LORD
(FEBRUARY 2)

Priest/Leader

"My eyes have seen your salvation,
which you have prepared in the presence of
all peoples."
God's powerful word
nourishes us on the feast of the Lord's Presentation.
We now turn to our God for what we need.

1. For joy in the Lord's presence.
(pause)
The prophet Malachi promised
that the Lord would come among the people.
May we welcome the Lord's presence among us,
challenging, correcting,
and comforting all the people of God.
Lord, hear us.

2. For trust in Christ our High Priest.
(pause)
Jesus is the High Priest,
our brother who shares our flesh and blood.
May we grow in faith each day,
trusting his power to save us
from the slavery of sin and death.
Lord, hear us.

3. For a desire to be consecrated to God.
(pause)
The Holy Family obeyed the traditions of
their people,
presenting the child in the Temple of the Lord.
May we be aware that we too are a consecrated
people,
called to God's service,
for the glory of all the nations.
Lord, hear us.

4. For openness to God's purposes.
(pause)
Jesus is declared by Simeon
a sign that will be rejected.
May we be open to God's mysterious purposes,
looking for the gift of wisdom
to live always by the gospel.
Lord, hear us.

Priest/Leader

God of the promises,
your Son is the light of all the nations.
Help us to be his faithful witnesses
and grant what we need
through Christ our Lord. Amen.

ST. JOSEPH
(MARCH 19)

Priest/Leader

We celebrate God's faithfulness
on the feast of St. Joseph.
Strengthened by God's word
and the example of St. Joseph,
we bring our needs before our God.

1. For an openness to God's purposes.
(pause)
God promised David
to preserve his offspring forever.
Like David, may we be open to God's purposes,
trusting in God's promise
to be with us always.
Lord, hear us.

2. For a deeper faith in God's goodness.
(pause)
Abraham is our father in faith,
and Joseph too put his faith in God.
As children of Abraham and with Joseph as our
patron,
may we also grow in faith
in the One who brings the dead to life.
Lord, hear us.

3. For the grace to act justly.
(pause)
Joseph is the just man
who constantly looked to do God's will.
May we be people of the gospel,
eager to witness to its teaching,
acting justly as God commands.
Lord, hear us.

4. For the gift of humility.
(pause)
Joseph is the model of humility,

living with righteousness the law of the Lord.
May we learn from his example
to live with integrity
in the service of our God.
Lord, hear us.

Priest/Leader

God of our ancestors,
we bless you on this feast of Joseph.
Grant what we need this day
through Christ our Lord. Amen.

ANNUNCIATION OF THE LORD
(MARCH 25)

Priest/Leader

"Let it be to me according to your word."
Today we celebrate the Annunciation
    of the Lord.
God's word has nourished us,
and with renewed confidence
we bring before the Lord all our needs.

1. For a spirit of thanksgiving.
(pause)
The maiden with child
is a sign of God's faithfulness.
May we be always thankful
to our God who is Immanuel:
God with us forever.
Lord, hear us.

2. For a desire to do God's will.
(pause)
Christ is our High Priest
whose obedience in sacrifice
has taken away our sins.
Like him, may we too sacrifice ourselves,
desiring to live as God wants.
Lord, hear us.

3. For a spirit of wonder.
(pause)
Mary was troubled and confused
by the message of the angel.
Like her, may we be open to God's purposes,
ready to accept God's will

in a spirit of obedience and wonder.
Lord, hear us.

4. For joy in celebrating God's good news.
(pause)
May we be filled with joy in the Annunciation
and moved by God's generosity.
May our lives so witness
to the good news of Jesus
that others may come to share our faith and joy.
Lord, hear us.

Priest/Leader

God of wonder,
you fill us with joy
in the good news of the Annunciation.
Grant what we need this day
through Christ our Lord. Amen.

BIRTH OF JOHN THE BAPTIST
(JUNE 24)

Priest/Leader

"The LORD called me before I was born."
John the Baptist prepared the way of the Lord.
Strengthened by God's powerful word
and the example of John the Baptist,
we bring our needs before our God.

1. For a desire to be servants of God.
(pause)
Scripture teaches us
that God calls us to service
even before we are born.
May we be good servants of the Lord
for the salvation of all the world.
Lord, hear us.

2. For a desire to turn from sin.
(pause)
John the Baptist is the herald of Christ,
proclaiming repentance to prepare his way.
May we learn from his example
to turn from sin in our lives
and welcome the coming of the Lord.
Lord, hear us.

3. For an awareness of God's kindness.
(pause)
God choose Elizabeth and Zechariah
to fulfill the ancient promises.
May we be open to God's purposes in life,
rejoicing in God's choices
and joyful in witnessing to God's ways.
Lord, hear us.

4. For the gift of patience.
(pause)
John lived in the wilderness,
patiently waiting for the Lord's call.
May we too be patient in God's service,
proclaiming God's promises among us
by the integrity of our lives.
Lord, hear us.

Priest/Leader

God of the promises,
we thank you for the witness of John the Baptist.
Help us to be good servants like him
and grant what we need
through Christ our Lord. Amen.

SAINTS PETER AND PAUL (JUNE 29)

Priest/Leader

"I will give you the keys of the kingdom of heaven."
We have been comforted by God's word
on this festival of Peter and Paul.
We turn to God with confidence
in our prayer for the church and the world.

1. For courage to witness to the gospel.
(pause)
May we share the confidence of Peter
in witnessing to the gospel,
certain of God's power to save
and sustained by the prayers
of the people of God.
Lord, hear us.

2. For courage to persevere until the end.
(pause)
May we be constant in fighting the good fight,

seeking God's purposes
for the church and the world.
May we be inspired by the example of Paul,
who persevered in faith to the end.
Lord, hear us.

3. For a deep faith in Jesus.
(pause)
Peter was declared blessed
for confessing Jesus as God's Messiah.
May we too be strong in faith,
acknowledging Jesus as the Christ,
the Son of the living God.
Lord, hear us.

4. For those who are leaders in the churches.
(pause)
Like Peter and Paul,
may Christian leaders be strong in faith.
May they be people of integrity,
alert to the signs of the times
in proclaiming the good news of the Lord.
Lord, hear us.

Priest/Leader

God of all ages,
we praise you for the witness of Peter and Paul.
Grant the prayers we make this day
through Christ our Lord. Amen.

INDEPENDENCE DAY (JULY 4)

Priest/Leader

"Seek the things that are above."
On this celebration of our independence,
God's word reminds us where our priorities must lie.
Encouraged by its teaching,
we turn to our God for what we need.

1. For a deep sense of thanksgiving.
(pause)
On our Independence Day,
may we acknowledge the blessings of God
on our country and its people,
longing for God's face to shine on us
and grant us God's peace.
Lord, hear us.

2. For a sense of urgency about doing God's will.
(pause)
On our Independence Day,
may we be filled with a sense of urgency,
aware of the shortness of our lives
and of the scripture teaching
to surrender our lives to God alone.
Lord, hear us.

3. For a desire to do God's will.
(pause)
On our Independence Day,
may we listen to the gospel teaching,
not pursuing things that fade
but constant in seeking to do God's will
as one people under God.
Lord, hear us.

4. For an attitude of thanksgiving to God.
(pause)
On our Independence Day,
may we be grateful to our God
for security, freedom, and peace,
seeking God's way of holiness
for our nation and for ourselves.
Lord, hear us.

Priest/Leader

God of all consolation,
we thank you for your many gifts
to our nation and our people.
May your kingdom come among us.
We ask this through Christ our Lord. Amen.

THE TRANSFIGURATION (AUGUST 6)

Priest/Leader

"This is my Son, the Beloved; listen to him."
God's word nourishes us
on this feast of the Transfiguration of Jesus.
Comforted by its message,
we bring our needs before our God.

1. For an awareness of the majesty of God's
      chosen one.
(pause)
The Book of Daniel teaches us

about the majesty of the Son of man.
On the feast of the Transfiguration
may we acknowledge the majesty of Jesus,
confessing him as the Holy One of God.
Lord, hear us.

2. For a renewed trust in God.
(pause)
Peter confesses that Jesus
has been glorified by God.
May we be given the grace
to deepen our trust in God's faithfulness
to be for us light in the darkness.
Lord, hear us.

3. For faith in Jesus, Son of God.
(pause)
Jesus is God's Son, the beloved.
May we be open to the message of his word,
listening to his teaching
and renewing our confidence
in the one who enjoys God's favor.
Lord, hear us.

4. For faith in God's kindness.
(pause)
On this feast of the Transfiguration of
      the Lord,
may we grow in understanding God's goodness
      and kindness;
and may we overcome fear in our lives,
recalling the resurrection of God's Son
and his triumph over evil and death.
Lord, hear us.

Priest/Leader

God of our ancestors,
you are faithful in every age.
Grant what we need to be your faithful people
through Christ our Lord. Amen.

THE ASSUMPTION (AUGUST 15)

Priest/Leader

"The last enemy to be destroyed is death."
Today we celebrate Christ's victory over sin and
      death,

and the assumption of the Virgin Mary, a great sign
    of that victory.
Confident that we too share that promise,
we turn to the Lord in prayer.

1. For hope in God's promises.
(*pause*)
Christ has been raised, the firstfruits
of those who have fallen asleep.
May we be filled with confidence in God's power,
and be assured that we too will share
the glory that has been promised.
Lord, hear us.

2. For the gift of thanksgiving.
(*pause*)
Mary is the woman, adorned by the sun,
standing on the moon, a crown of stars on
    her head.
May we be thankful to God
that she is also the faithful one,
who lived always to do God's will.
Lord, hear us.

3. For a desire to imitate Mary in our lives.
(*pause*)
Mary proclaimed the greatness of the Lord
to her cousin Elizabeth.
May she be for us a constant example
of the way of Christ
by her openness to God and her care for others.
Lord, hear us.

4. For a renewed faith in God's plan for our lives.
(*pause*)
God chose Mary to be the mother of the Savior,
and we too have a place in God's plan of salvation.
May we be faithful followers of Christ
that, by Mary's prayers,
we may share the glory of the resurrection.
Lord, hear us.

Priest/Leader

God of all creation,
you raised Mary to glory
and she is our queen and mother.
Listen to our prayers this day
through Christ our Lord. Amen.

LABOR DAY

Priest/Leader

"Do not worry about tomorrow,
for tomorrow will bring worries of its own."
The gospel for Labor Day commands us to trust
in God's goodness.
Strengthened by its teaching,
we approach our God with humility
for what we need in the church and in the
    community.

1. For an awareness of the dignity of work.
(*pause*)
God is the author of all good things,
and the Earth is God's gift to us.
May we acknowledge the worth of our labor,
sharing with delight in the creation
and caring for what God has made.
Lord, hear us.

2. For a right attitude to our work.
(*pause*)
Paul commands us to live according to
    his teaching.
May we have a right attitude to our work,
avoiding laziness, idleness, and selfishness
and aware of the needs of others
in our families and communities.
Lord, hear us.

3. For a desire to work for God's kingdom.
(*pause*)
May we look for balance in our lives.
seeking God's way of holiness
and trusting our lives and our work
to the goodness and kindness of our God,
who knows all that we need.
Lord, hear us.

4. For a desire to put God first.
(*pause*)
May our celebration of Labor Day
help us reflect on our lives
and to acknowledge the greatness of God
as we work for the coming of the kingdom
in our families, our communities, and our nation.
Lord, hear us.

Priest/Leader

God of all creation,
we thank you for your loving-kindness.
Teach us the way of holiness,
for you are Lord, forever and ever. Amen.

ALL SAINTS (NOVEMBER 1)

Priest/Leader

"Blessed are the poor in spirit."
The word has been broken for us
on this feast of all God's holy ones.
With confidence, we turn to our God
for what we need.

1. For the grace to live by the gospel.
(pause)
Like all the saints of God,
may we be faithful witnesses to the gospel;
and, like them, may we be numbered
among God's chosen ones
who live by the teaching of the Lamb.
Lord, hear us.

2. For joy in living as God's children.
(pause)
May we be filled with joy,
thankful to our God
who has lavished love upon us,
declaring us God's children,
filled with hope in the promises of God.
Lord, hear us.

3. For a desire to live as God wants.
(pause)
May we be the people of the Beatitudes,
taking its teaching to our hearts,
and living out its values
by lives of integrity,
honesty, and love.
Lord, hear us.

4. For God's people everywhere.
(pause)
On this feast of All Saints,
we pray for all the people of God.

May they be kingdom people,
declared blessed by God,
eager to follow Christ's teaching.
Lord, hear us.

Priest/Leader

God of all saints, we bless you and thank you
for their lives and witness.
Help us to live as faithful disciples of your Son,
who is Lord forever and ever. Amen.

ALL SOULS (NOVEMBER 2)

Priest/Leader

"I know that he will rise again
in the resurrection on the last day."
We worship our God on this feast of All Souls
and bring before the Lord our concerns,
our needs, and our memories.

1. For a firm faith in the promises of God.
(pause)
May we renew our faith in our God,
who has been faithful to the ancient promises,
and with a firm trust in God's goodness
commend ourselves and those who have died
to God's loving care.
Lord, hear us.

2. For hope in the resurrection.
(pause)
Jesus has promised to raise us up
on the last day.
May we be filled with hope in the resurrection
promised to us
and to all who believe in him.
Lord, hear us.

3. For those who have died.
(pause)
We pray for those who have died
in the blessed hope of resurrection
that they may see God
in whom they believed
and enjoy God's presence forever.
Lord, hear us.

4. For those who mourn.
(*pause*)
May those who are in mourning
and grieving for those who have died
be comforted by their faith and hope
and by the loving care of others
in the church and in the community.
Lord, hear us.

Priest/Leader

God of all ages,
to you a thousand years is like a day.
Be close to us as we recall our dead.
Comfort us with your gifts of faith and hope.
We ask this through Christ our Lord. Amen.

THANKSGIVING DAY

Priest/Leader

"One's life does not consist
in the abundance of possessions."
On Thanksgiving Day,
we acknowledge God's blessings
and the bounty of our land.
In a spirit of thanksgiving,
we approach our God for what
     we need.

1. For a deeper awareness of God's goodness.
(*pause*)
May we gladly acknowledge the goodness
     of our God
and the many gifts we receive
at God's hands,
recalling the kindness God has shown
to our communities and to our nation.
Lord, hear us.

2. For an attitude of thanksgiving
     in our lives.
(*pause*)
May we be people who give thanks
for the favor of God
and the fellowship of Christ.
May our strength be in the gospel
and our lives witnesses to its teaching.
Lord, hear us.

3. For a sense of what is important in life.
(*pause*)
As a nation and as a community,
may we know what is of ultimate value in life,
not consumed by a desire for wealth
but eager to live by the gospel
through lives of moderation and gentleness.
Lord, hear us.

4. For a desire to be rich in God's sight.
(*pause*)
As God's people in God's world,
may we learn from the example of Jesus,
who lived not for himself but for others;
and may we so live by his teaching
to be rich in the sight of God.
Lord, hear us.

Priest/Leader

God of the promises,
you are generous in your gifts to us.
Help us to be faithful disciples of Jesus
in our nation and our communities.
We ask this through Christ our Lord. Amen.

IMMACULATE CONCEPTION
(DECEMBER 8)

Priest/Leader

"Greetings, favored one! The Lord is with you."
We rejoice in the Immaculate Conception
of the Blessed Virgin Mary
and bring our needs before our God.

1. For a spirit of thankfulness.
(*pause*)
Even when our first parents sinned,
God promised that the woman would triumph
     over evil.
May we be thankful this day
for Mary of Nazareth,
whom God chose to be the mother of the Savior.
Lord, hear us.

2. For a deep trust in God's love.
(*pause*)
The scripture teaches us

about the faithfulness of God
from the beginning of time.
May we grow in trust of our loving God,
who blesses us in Christ to be adopted children,
    God's own people.
Lord hear us.

3. For a desire to live as God wants.
(pause)
Mary was disturbed by the angel's message
but trusted God's message of good news.
Like her, may we be open to God's purposes;
and may we be ready to accept God's will
in a spirit of obedience and wonder.
Lord, hear us.

4. For joy in celebrating God's good news.
(pause)
May we be filled with joy in this festival
and moved by God's generosity.
May we live lives
that so reflect gospel teaching
that others may come to share our faith and joy.
Lord, hear us.

Priest/Leader

God of all consolation,
we bless you on this festival of Mary.
Grant what we need this day,
for we make our prayer in Jesus' name. Amen.